SOLDIER OF THE LEAF

SOLDIER OF THE LEAF

Marvin E. Brown
PROFESSIONAL SKATE GUARD CHIEF:

A PARK SUPERVISOR
RETIRED

authorHOUSE®

AuthorHouse™
1663 Liberty Drive
Bloomington, IN 47403
www.authorhouse.com
Phone: 1-800-839-8640

Published by AuthorHouse   10/04/2012

ISBN: 978-1-4772-6090-6 (sc)
ISBN: 978-1-4772-6089-0 (e)

Library of Congress Control Number: 2012914855

DEDICATED
TO MOM, MAMA ALICE AND RITA

I SHED A TEAR
I shed a tear for you, mother
I shed a tear for you
I cry I'm sad my life is empty
I feel the pain through and through
I said a prayer for you, mother
I prayed and prayed for you
I asked the Lord to receive you
Your work on Earth is through.
I'll miss you so darling mother
I'll miss your warm sweet touch
Until we meet in the morning
At Heaven's gate in our glory
I'll say farewell to you, mother
I'll say goodbye to you
I love you so, my heart is breaking
Go take your place among the angels
R.I.P.

My earliest childhood memories are from three years of age, when I was three years old. I lived with my grandparents on their farm in Cairo, GA. (Grady County). My grandfather brought me to the farm when I was two years old. My mother lost her job in Jacksonville, FL and couldn't take care of me. One day, my grandfather took me with him into town on his wagon, which was pulled by two mules. Their names were "Rock and Nell." Rock was a tall and proud looking red mule, high strung, and she had a black stripe down the middle of her back from her mane to the end of her tail. She was also very high spirited. Nell, who was solid, had a black coat which glistened in the sun. She had a more relaxed demeanor and was much easier to handle. My grandfather parked the wagon near the train depot. While granddaddy was in the store having a sack of corn ground into grits and corn meal, my cousin and I were waiting in the wagon. All of a sudden there was something coming down the road making such a noise like I had never heard before. There were bells ringing and smoke (steam) blowing in every direction. It made a scary huffing and puffing sound. There was black smoke coming from a stovepipe, which protruded from the top of it. It had huge iron wheels on each side and a loud whistle was blowing. Whatever it was, it was coming to get me. I wanted to jump out the wagon and run away but my cousin who was a little older would not turn me loose. I found a way to hide inside the wagon, and that's what I did until the monster rumbled past and was out of sight. When granddaddy returned, I was only too happy to be heading back home. I had just encountered my first railroad train.

One day granddaddy was hauling wood and tree stumps from down in the branch to be used at the sugar mill during cane grinding time when we would make syrup. I went out to the sugar mill to watch him work. I was standing on one of the tree stumps that he had thrown off the wagon. He stopped what he was doing and stared down at me from the wagon for a minute then he said "ain't that a snake you're standing on?" And sure enough, it was. It had red, black and yellow bands around it. It was a pretty little coral snake and very deadly. It takes three drops of cobra venom to equal one drop of coral snake venom. Fortunately for me, granddaddy had killed it with the ax without even knowing it. He didn't even see it until I was standing on it.

One day, as I was sitting on the ditch bank alongside the road that went past our house playing in the sand, I realized that I was being stung all over. I was sitting in an ant bed and they had crawled all over my body. They began stinging me all at the same time. I ran to grandma. She removed all my clothes and gave me a bath in the foot tub. Afterwards, I was covered with blisters.

Late one night, we were all awakened by lots of gun fire. The shooting was being done by the local Ku Klux Klan, who paid us a visit to discourage my grandparents and other black people from voting. My grandfather was involved with the school board and the education of black children who attended school in a degraded one-room school house which was actually the local church. It was also known as Cedar Springs School. This was in the mid 1940's and President Roosevelt wanted black people to vote. The Klan shot around the house. Granddaddy went out on the front porch to confront them. They ran Uncle Bud through the woods, still shooting their guns. They told granddaddy to send word to Mrs. Bee that there would be no school tomorrow. Our nearest neighbor was farmer Mr. Bill, who was also the Sheriff. He came down and ran them off. My granddaddy said he recognized the voice of his white neighbor farmer. Even with their sheets covering their faces, granddaddy said it was the white farmers and their crew of KKK men. President Roosevelt died and black people didn't get to vote until after the civil rights movement started for another 15 years.

Sugar cane harvesting starts in the fall, October and November. My grandparents and my uncle and cousin started working in the sugar cane field. First of all, the leaves are stripped from the cane then the tops are cut off, then the cane is cut down low to the ground and stacked in piles. Once the cutting is finished, Uncle Son cranks the stationary industrial engine that powers the mill and starts the milling and grinding process. Uncle Son spun the fly wheel around with a crank. When the engine fires the first time, a flame jumps out of the exhaust pipe and reaches all the way to the ceiling. It stands on the exhaust pipe until the fly wheel makes a complete revolution and the second time it fires, it blows out the flame. This whole scenario was frightening as it was fascinating to a three and a half year old. Uncle Son then climbs up on the platform where the cane has been stacked after it was hauled by a mule and wagon from the field by my cousin. Uncle Son feeds the cane through the mill where the juice is squeezed out of the cane. The juice is then piped from the trough that catches it from the mill into an open vacuum pan where it snakes its way from one end to the other. My grandmother stands there and skims off all the impurities which boil up as foam. There is a blazing furnace underneath the vacuum pan. After the juice reaches the far end, it has been condensed into syrup. There it drains off into a 30-gallon barrel. After it's all finished, the barrels are taken into town and sold to a company that processes it into raw sugar.

The month of January is hog killing time. On the coldest day of the year, my grandfather and Uncle Son would kill around 12 hogs and butcher them and hang the meat in the smoke house where it is cured. This provides us with meat and lard, sausage, souse and crackling skins for the year.

I went to school in a one-room school house in the Cedar Springs AME Church which was about a mile and a half from our farm. The teacher was my aunt. She taught all the black children from the surrounding farm community. The grades were first through the eighth. From the ninth grade up, you had to go to school in town. Mrs. Bee would line every one up for spelling and if you misspelled a word, you had to hold out your hand. She then spelled out each letter as she whacked your hand with a hickory stick. She only had to do that to me once. After that, I always made sure I knew everything. I was a straight "A" student. Then one day they made us go to school in town. I didn't learn anything. The teacher in town gave me an assignment. If you did well or not, the teachers gave you a passing grade.

My cousin and I were walking to school one morning and I wanted to impress everybody with my new sling shot that I made the day before. I shot holes in the eggs which were in a nest on the ditch bank alongside the road. Well, the hen and the eggs belonged to Mrs. Daisy Bogan the mother of my two friends. My cousins raced to the school house to tell Mrs. Bee who went out in the woods and got a new hickory stick to beat me with. She chased me under every desk and table. I was trying desperately to get away from her. When I got home from school, my grandfather was waiting for me with the plow line off of Nell's gear. I thought he would beat me within an inch of my life.

It was the first week in November 1957 when two friends and I decided to hitchhike to New York. We tried to join the circus but they wouldn't have us. We were three 14 year old boys from the south trying to join the circus to see the world. So early one morning, Bill, Rudolph and I left Savannah, Georgia walking north on highway 17. After we had gone a few miles into South Carolina, we decided to split up as we weren't getting any rides. There were too many of us, so Bill and Rudolph stayed together and left me to go alone.

We were supposed to meet in Brooklyn where Rudolph's uncle was the super in a building at 386 Ocean Parkway. We were going to live in the basement. I had no idea what any of that meant. A schoolteacher picked me up and took me as far as Sumpter, S.C. where he was going to attend a teacher's conference. It was still daylight so I got out of the car and started walking north on highway US 1. After I got tired of walking, it was very dark so I crawled up under a railroad track bridge and tried to get to sleep. The mosquitoes ate me alive all night.

I must have fallen to sleep because the next thing I knew, there was hammering going on above my head on the railroad tracks.

The railroad workers were working on the tracks. I crawled out to the road and began walking. I had 75 cents given to me by the school teacher. I bought something to eat and continued walking with my thumb out. I was picked-up a few times but the rides weren't very long. The temperature was getting colder, but I didn't feel it too much as I was wearing all my clothes. I was wearing two pair of pants, three shirts, two coats and two pairs of socks. By nightfall, I made it to the North Carolina State Line. I came to a crossroad. It was pitch-black dark. I heard a bobcat scream from deep in the woods. I had no idea, which way I should go, when in the distance, I saw a pair of headlights approaching. An old pick-up truck came to a stop. Two middle-age men were riding in the truck. One of them asked me, "Boy, what in the world are you doing out here in the middle of the woods by yourself?"

"I'm on my way to New York," I replied. I think you'd better come with us before one of those wild cats get you. One of the men got out and allowed me to climb in the truck and sit between the two of them. "My name's Willie Jay and I run a liquor business in this town." "What town is this?" I asked. "This is Rockingham, North Carolina." We rode on until we past the woods, and I began to see houses. Willie Jay stopped at one of the houses and the man in the passenger seat got out and said, "Good night."

We drove on until we came to his house. He parked his truck and we got out and went inside. He introduced me to his wife who placed a blanket on the couch and told me to sleep there for the night. Early the next morning around seven o'clock, Willie Jay drove me out to the highway. He pointed straight ahead and said New York is that way. I got out of the truck and started walking;

putting out my thumb each time a car went by. After a couple of hours, a car stopped. I got in the car which was driven by a U.S. Marine who was on his way from Paris Island, South Carolina to Quantico, Virginia. He gave me a ride to Fredericksburg, Virginia and bought me a ticket on the Greyhound Bus to New York. I arrived at the 34th street bus station at 3:30 on Thursday morning. It only took me three days. It would be several weeks before I saw Bill and Rudolph again.

So now, I'm sitting in the bus station trying to figure out where Ocean Parkway was and how do I get there. A man in a uniform came over and started asking me questions about who I was with and where did I come from and that I looked like a runaway. He indicated that I should remain where I was while he went looking for a police officer to take me to some kind of home for runaways. I had no intention of going to any such place. As soon as he was out of sight, I went out of the side door. I went into the subway station and asked how to get to Ocean Parkway. The man in the booth told me to take the BMT Brighton Beach train and get off at the Ocean Parkway stop.

I got off the train and walked along Ocean Parkway to look for the building where Rudolph's uncle lived, but the numbers were too high. So, I got back on the train and didn't get off for two days. I rode the subway line from one end to the other—sleeping most of the time. The next evening, I decided to try again to find 386 Ocean Parkway. It was snowing and very cold. I started walking and the farther I walked, the building's numbers became smaller and smaller. After walking for two hours, I came to 386 Ocean Parkway. I went through a very large glass doors into the lobby.

There were about 10 or 15 doors in the hallway. Which one belonged to Rudolph's uncle? I knocked on the first door I came to. A man opened the door and yelled at me "You, banging on my door, I'm calling the police." You are supposed to ring the door bell, but I didn't know that. I left running. As I walked slowly back to the subway station it was snowing very heavily. I searched each garbage can for food as I walked along the sidewalk, occasionally I found scraps of bread to eat. When I got back to the subway station, I was soaking wet and freezing cold. I sat on the floor in a corner. After a few minutes, a policeman came in the station from one of the trains. The token clerk must have called him. He called me over to where he was and started asking who I was and where I came from. He said I should take off my coat and place it over the radiator to dry. The policeman asked people who were leaving the subway if they knew me. I told him that I came from down South and didn't know anyone here, nor did anyone know me. After about 30 minutes, the policeman took me on the train two stops to the Sheepshead Bay Station.

There we went into a restaurant and he bought me soup and a sandwich. Before I could finish eating, one of the people who were leaving the subway came into the restaurant and told the officer I was his cousin. Afterwards, the man told me his name was Richard and took me home with him.

Richard said, if he hadn't rescued me, the policeman would have taken me to a jail for children. Richard lived in a rooming house with his wife. So, the only place I could sleep was in the kitchen by placing all the chairs together. I could lie down on them and sleep there which was a little more comfortable than sleeping on the subway. Early the next morning, Richard left for work. I was still trying to get comfortable on the chairs when the door opened and a woman who appeared to be old enough to be my grandmother came into the kitchen and started screaming at me. "You get out of here and stop burning my lights." I jumped up and left running as fast as I could go as she was very angry. I ran across the street and waited for her to leave. I then went back into the house for it was very cold and the snow was very deep. No sooner was I back in the kitchen, the door swung open and she came storming back. "Didn't I tell you to get out of here and stop burning my lights?" I ran out again, but this time I went around the corner and waited a long time after she was gone, before I returned to the kitchen. After it got dark, a man came into the house and said, "Hello son, my name is George. What's your name?" "Marvin" I replied. "Well tell me Marvin, where are you from and how did you end up here?" "I hitch-hiked up from Savannah, Georgia and Richard brought me here from the subway." "Well do you have any relatives here?" "No sir. I don't know anybody." "Alright" said George. "I'll tell you what; I have a couple of rooms upstairs. You can go up and sleep in one of those rooms. Pick any one you like. When you get hungry, come down to my house and eat. I live at 470 Neptune Ave. You can stay here as long as you like. Just don't cause any trouble." "Thank you, sir." "How old are you?" "I'm 18, sir." "You sure look young for 18."

The next day, I went to George's house to eat. I knocked on the door and it opened and there stood a young boy who looked a couple of years younger than me. He looked me up and down. "You must be Marvin." Before I could answer he said, "You came here to eat didn't you? My name is David," he said as I walked into the apartment and this is my sister Princess." He pointed to a girl who was doing school work from a book in her room, just down the hall. He led me to the kitchen. He said "Mama Alice is waiting for you." "Sit down over here. I've made you bacon and eggs and toast." The angry woman who chased me from the kitchen yesterday is Mama Alice who is actually cooking breakfast for me in a different kitchen. Today she was treating me very nice. "Do you want orange juice or coffee? You don't look old enough to be drinking coffee. I'm giving you orange juice. Are you sure you're18 years old?" "Yes ma'am, I'm 18." "After you finish eating, I think you should go look for a job," said Mama Alice. "I don't know where to look," I told her. "Try the Brighton laundry factory around the corner." I walked around to the large building, went inside to the personnel office and inquired about a job and was hired. With the Christmas season approaching they needed more people. So I now had a job. The pay was $40.00 per week and my work hours were 7:00 a.m. to 4:00 p.m., starting tomorrow morning.

My job was sorting through metal number tags which were used to mark the laundry bag. What a tedious and boring job. I wrote home to let my mother know where I was. She wrote back to me that she needed money. So, I sent her a $50.00 dollar bill. She told her neighbor, who then told the housing office. The Housing Office evicted her from the apartment. We lived in a project called Yamacraw Village. When you receive extra money, you are supposed to let them know, so they can increase your rent. Christmas was coming up. I had been working at the laundry for a month. I went shopping for a gift for everybody in the house. They weren't very big gifts, but everyone liked them. After

Christmas I was laid off. George told me to pack my things as he was going to drive me to the bus station and I should go back home. He said, I should come back when I was older. Everyone kept telling me, I looked rather young to be 18 years old and they were right. I was only 15. I arrived in Savannah and took a cab to Yamacraw Village.

There were no lights on and the door was locked. There didn't seem to be anyone home. The next door neighbor came out to tell me that my family had moved to some place on the other side of Bay Street. I walked the half a mile to Bay Street. After I crossed to the other side, there was a line of old row houses. Most of them were abandoned. After inquiring, someone directed me to one of the houses and there I found my mother and five younger brothers. She had just had a new baby born on my birthday, Nov.15, a baby boy who she named Randy. He was born with one tooth in his mouth which had a hole through it. The rooms had many of the boards missing from the floor. You had to be very careful where you stepped as you could end up under the house. I had some money saved so I bought a newspaper the next morning and searched the want ads and found an apartment in another part of town. The rent was $9 a month and it cost $7 to get someone to move us. I didn't stay in Savannah very long.

I got a job passing out hand bills to all the cars coming from the North as they passed under the railroad over pass on Louisville Road. The hand bills advertised a restaurant which was located a little farther South along highway 17. I left after a couple of months and returned to Cairo to my grandfather's farm. He was a little surprised to see me. I told him that I wasn't coming back, because farming was not for me. After helping grandpa plant the crops during the spring, I moved into town and started working for the American Tobacco Co. They grew shade tobacco in Havana and Quincy, Fla. My pay was 40 cents an hour or $4.00 a day. After the tobacco season was over, I went to Orlando with Curtis Miller, a good friend who had an uncle who was a plasterer and worked for a building contractor. He was building new homes in Kissimee. Fla., which at that time was just a large orange grove. We got jobs working with the contracting crew. Curtis' job was mixing the plaster. My job was to carry the plaster to the plasterer and to do it fast enough so that they didn't run out of plaster. Only thing was, I was spending more time eating oranges and grapefruits. When they ran out of plaster, they would start yelling for me to hurry and bring more. Well, I got fired for eating on company time. After that, I ended up in Miami for a couple of months. I lived with my cousin Joe Marion and cousin Grace Everett, who was a very beautiful lady, to my 16 year-old eyes. She was from Mississippi. I would drive her to sell her Avon products. She couldn't drive the standard shift Buick which cousin Joe used for a work car.

Three days before Christmas, my cousins Joe and Grace took me back to my grandfather in Cairo and left me there. After we prepared the fields for planting in the spring and after planting, I left and moved to town and started working on a tobacco farm. I worked all summer in tobacco in Havana and Quincy, Fla. At the end of August, the foreman Bobby Willis took two bus loads of workers to Windsor, Connecticut to work in tobacco there. Tobacco grew twice as tall as in Florida and we had to stand on 4' benches in order to reach the top leaves. Everybody lived in a tobacco barn which was outfitted with bunk beds. After six weeks, everybody went home except me and Curtis Miller. We remained in Hartford for a month after which I took a greyhound bus to New York. My first stop after leaving Hartford Conn. was Newark, New Jersey.

There I lived for a week with my grandmother's cousins Bertha and Arlie Akins. During that week, cousin Bertha arranged for me to work on a moving van. When it was time to unload the furniture, each man would carry an appliance on his back. One man carried the Singer sewing machine on his back. I was supposed to carry the refrigerator on my back. But when they strapped the refrigerator on my back and shoved it off the back of the truck, I went down to the ground with the refrigerator on top of me. The boss didn't think I would fit in too well. I agreed and headed for Brooklyn and was reunited with my New York adopted family and old friends, the Hitt Family and Mama Alice.

I was welcomed by my New York family and the following week, I found a job as a messenger at the Atlantic Electro Type Company. They made engraving plates for all the advertising agencies, newspapers and magazines all over the city. My job was to deliver them to the various newspapers and agencies around the city. The shipping clerk was my boss. His name was Frank and he gave me $30.00 for carfare. My weekly pay was $40.00 a week, which was double what I made working in the tobacco fields back home.

When walking from East 45th Street, sometimes I would see Jackie Robinson crossing 3rd Ave. He was the President of Chock

Full of Nuts Coffee. He was also from Cairo, Ga. In fact, he was my grandmother's first cousin. So one day, I went up to him and introduced myself and told him I was from Cairo, Ga. He said to me, "Well, I'm from there too, but it was a long time ago." I learned later that his parents left Cairo and moved to California when he was only 3 years old.

One day, Mr. Martin Beck, who was the owner of Atlantic Electro Type, the place where I worked, decided to fire the salesman who brought in all the big accounts. Mr. Beck figured if he dismissed the salesman, he wouldn't have to pay him a commission. Well, the salesman went over to another electro type company and took all the big accounts with him. Atlantic Electro Type went downhill from there. Pretty soon I had to look for another job.

Whenever I was waiting for the elevator, I would be singing in the hallway. A couple who ran the printing company heard me singing and arranged for me to have an audition with Decca Records. Their company printed album covers for Decca. Well, I went over to Park Ave. and sang a song for the A&R director who had a piano player to accompany me. As the piano player played, I wasn't keeping time with the music. I was told afterwards that I had a good voice but I needed to get more experience.

I started singing in amateur shows in Harlem and Brooklyn. After all, I really came to New York to be a rock and roll singer. I made a number of demos at Bell Round Studios and left them at different record companies. They said, "Don't call us, we'll call you." Someone told me it's not what you know, it's who you know. It took a while before I understood what that meant. In any case, my rock and roll career never took off. After I left Atlantic Electro Type, I found a job at a company in Long Island City that made portable hair dryers. My job was to operate the injection molding machine which injected hot 800-degree liquid plastic into a dye that formed the outer housing for the hair dryer. One day, one of the other workers got his hand caught in the injector. It closed on his hand and when it opened, three of his fingers were hanging by a piece of skin. He was bleeding profusely. The foreman asked me to escort the man to the first-aid room which was a block away from where we worked. I left him there. I didn't know what his fate was until a few days later.

I was offered a job as an electrician's helper in Sheepshead Bay. An electrician friend of Mama Alice needed a younger man to do the harder work such as carrying a roll of box cable or climbing the ladder. The first few months, I was his helper. I learned to install circuit breakers panels and meters and run ac outlets and hang light fixtures. After I had learned enough, he was my helper, as I was doing most of the work, as well as, all of the driving,

On New Year's Day 1961, David, Princess and I were walking through Prospect Park when we came upon a new ice skating rink. We got on the long line of people and went into the place and rented ice skates. I was really fascinated with the idea of ice skating, having come from a farm in southwest Georgia. I had never seen an ice rink before. It was something I never imagined myself doing. The moment I stepped onto the ice, I fell flat on my face. I got up and fell down again. So I held onto the railing until I could stand up on my own. Before the session was over, I could actually ice skate. So the very next day, I went out and bought a pair of ice skates and went skating every night for the next two weeks. A fellow named Ray Scott offered me a job as a skate guard. They're the people who skate around the ice and enforce the rules of the rink and carry away the skaters who get hurt on the ice. They also resurface the ice after the session is over.

Well, this job offer went on from 1961-1964. After much thought, I decided to take it. I went to the Prospect Park office and they told me they didn't need anybody, but if I went over to the Wollman Rink in Central Park, they might need somebody. I went to the Wollman Rink. I talked to a red-headed woman about getting hired and she said, "You'll have to wait for Mr. Ginkilla. He went to the Arsenal but he'll be back in an hour." So I waited. Sometime later a tall man called me into the office and said, "I understand you're looking for job as a skate guard." "Yes sir," I said. "Put your skates on and let me see how well you skate." So I skated around the ice a few times. Mr. Ginkilla called me into the office and said, "Ok you skate all right! I am going to take a chance and hire you. Take this slip of paper over to the Arsenal. Go into the basement and give it to the clerk." The paper read . . . "Please appoint Mr. Marvin Brown as a Seasonal Park Helper." I gave the clerk the slip of paper and she in turn gave me a stack of papers to fill out. I was finger-printed and paid fifteen cents to the finger-print man and was sent up to the second floor to see the Borough Clerk. I walked into his office. A little short man sat at a desk. He appeared to be hiding behind many tall stacks of papers which covered his desk. The papers were stack so high that you could not see the little man unless he stood up, which he did when I walked in. He yelled, "What do you want?" As I started to hand him my papers, he said to go wait out side in the hall, which I did. There were a few other guys sitting on a bench so I took a seat next to them. A couple of them introduced themselves to me. "Hi, I am Greg and this is Chino." I told them my name and Greg said, "I guess we are all going to be skate guards at the ice rink."

After an hour, Mr. Borough Clerk called us into his office, one at a time and had us sign our name in a very large book. He then gave each of us a large yellow button that had a number on it along with the words Seasonal Park Helper. We all returned to the rink and gave our yellow appointment slip to the red-headed woman whose name was Carmela. Mr. Ginkilla called us all together and said, "I want all you fellows to walk up to the Dairy Building and pick up your uniforms. The Dairy Building is a storage supply building. We collected our uniforms which consisted of a pair of blue trousers with a red stripe down the leg and a blue jacket with red trim around it. We also collected a blue shirt and black bow tie. In full uniform, we looked like a group of displaced doormen on an ice skating outing. Mr. Ginkella instructed us to start work at 8:00 a.m. the next morning in our skates and uniforms.

A fellow name George was drilling holes in the ice to find out how thick it was. He was going to be working all night spraying hot water on the ice to build it up so that by morning, it would be thicker. There has to be at least one half to three quarters inches thick of ice on the rink because on weekends, there are thousands of people skating and they could easily skate off half an inch. I would be working six days a week and paid $12.00 a day and have a day off during the week. I would be on the day crew which would consist of 12 guys and one chief. The night crew was made up the same way. They started work at 4:00 p.m.

I left for home and needless to say, I was quite excited over the coming Saturday. I set my clock to wake me up at 6:00 a.m. on Saturday morning. After not working all week, I was well rested and very energetic. When I arrived at the facility and entered the locker room, it was 7:00 a.m. and the only person there was Mr. Dolittle. "Hi, how are you?" "Ok," I said. "I notice the ice is covered with what looks to me like snow." "Yes, that's called frost . . . . before anyone can skate on it, we'll have to pan it off. Did you sign in?" "No," I said and he took me into the office and showed me where to sign in. "Here's where you sign in, always on the blotter that says, Seasonals. You write your title which is S P H, your name and then the time you came in." By this time a few others were coming in. I went in and put my skates on. Frank came in and put on a pair of skates and I asked him why he was doing that. I thought he only fixed things. "Oh I'm actually not supposed to be here today, but the boss felt that as I was one of the chiefs here for many years, I should be here to help the chief in showing the new guys what to do. I'm normally off Saturday, Sunday and holidays."

By 8:00 a.m., we were all going around the ice, one behind the other pushing a large snow-shovel called a pan and holding it in a tilted position so that each one moved the snow over a bit more than the person ahead of him, until the circle got smaller and smaller. Finally there were three or four piles of snow on various parts of the rink. Then, George Finlayson pushed the snow into the pit with the jeep. The pit is a small area in the corner of the rink which is built on the 59th street lake where there is always water running to melt the snow. It's also a good place to look for money and jewelry early in the morning after a heavy session the night before.

After we put away the pans, we were told to pull out the water hose which the chief used to spray the ice with hot water. The rest of us used large squeegees to push the water toward the front of the rink in much the same way as we skated from the back of the rink from one side to other, each man pushing the water a little farther toward the front of the rink. About half way, everyone was getting tired and began to slow down. The chief came over and said, "Alright you guys, it's 9:30 and if you stop to rest, this line of slush is going to freeze and leave one long streak across the ice, and if that happens, Ginkilla is going to come out here and raise hell and we'll have to take a cut." After this, everyone managed to get a little more life into themselves even though Jim Clifford grumbled, "What the hell does he want for $12 a day? I'm not going to kill myself."

After we finished squeegeeing and rolling up the hose, we all took off our skates and Walter Shumway led us to the zoo cafeteria for breakfast or coffee whichever we preferred. We returned after an hour. There was a small group of young girls skating on the ice. I learned that they were the figure & dance club and the best ones received special instructions from Von Gassner, who in turn accepted a substantial sum of money from the parents or grandparents of these young protégés for his services. He regarded skate guards as some form of low life, even though he depended on them to prepare the ice for his group. The Von, as he was referred to by us, had the ice every Saturday and holiday mornings from 9:00 a.m. till 10:00 a.m. After his session, there was a free session for school children up to and below the age of 14 years old. Meanwhile, there were a large number of kids gathering outside the fence on the bleachers.

At about a quarter to ten, we were all assembled in the locker room and at the instruction of the chief, put on our skates and full uniforms. We were given our final instructions. "Alright now, here's what you're going to do. While you patrol the ice, you're to keep them from sitting on and climbing over the rails. Don't let 'em skate against the flow of traffic and keep the little brats off Von Gassner in the center of the rink with his figure and dance students. No spinning and jumping is allowed and you gotta keep an eye on the parents and guardians. They aren't allowed on the ice. All kids on the ice must have skates on."

At 10 o'clock, we were all on the ice and George had a guard at the gate allowing only those kids in who were under 14 years old or who otherwise had proof of their age. You could ask, "What year were you born?" If they took too long to remember when they were born, they weren't allowed in because they would be lying anyway. The chief got on the public address system and read the rules and regulations. Meanwhile the kids were having such a good time.

They didn't seem to hear the announcement anyway. They were stumbling around, falling down and holding on to the rails but many of them skated very well. Meanwhile, Greg Johnson was standing on one spot talking to a young skater who was, I'd say at least 15 if not more. After about ten minutes, the supervisor was on the PA system. "Greg Johnson front and center." Chino and I skated around together and he started to tell me about his involvement with art. He attended a school call Art Students League and when he finished his course, he was going to be greater than Michelangelo.

Suddenly Greg darted past us and stopped. I inquired why he was called to the office and he said, "Old Cyclops told me not to be fraternizing with the public and I'd better get out there and do some work if I wanted to keep my job." Chino said, "Man, you know how to fraternize! Who have you been fraternizing with?" Greg answered. "Oh, it was only Millie the Phillie. She used to go swimming at my pool during the summer." I understood that Greg, Chino and a few others as well, worked as life guards during the summer and skate guards during the winter, and that a few others worked as filter plant operators, whatever that was.

During the course of the session a number of accidents occurred. There were cases where little kids would fall and before the kid could get up or before one of us could get to help him, some other kid would skate over his finger or hand. There was a case where a girl's finger was completely severed from her hand. We stopped the music and called everybody off the ice while we looked for the finger. We finally found the finger in the child's glove. She was taken to Roosevelt Hospital. We also had to put out many people who, although they insisted they were under 14, were obviously much older.

At 12 o'clock the free session ended and the speed session began. At this time, everybody was allowed to go to lunch except for one guy who was assigned to watch the speed session. The only thing he had to do was to keep the other kids who weren't members of the speed club, off the ice. The man in charge of the speed club yelled through a megaphone to the skaters.

"Who is he—the speed skating expert?" I asked. Greg said, "Aw, he's just a recreation director. He comes around on Saturday and does the speed skating session and while he's here, he signs the blotter for the whole week and on pay-day he comes in and picks up his check. In other words, he gets about $200 an hour. You wouldn't believe how many people are milking the city. Meanwhile, we have to get out there and bust our asses for $12 a day. But that's nothing. All the recreation leaders have been doing it for years."

I remarked that I didn't think our job was so bad. "Oh, yeah," Greg said. "Man you ain't seen nothing yet. Wait until it snows, then we're going to separate the men from the boys." At 1 o'clock, we had our skates on and were back on the ice. The jeep was hooked to the cutter which is an iron and steel machine, built with a steel blade, about 2 inches thick, 5 inches wide and 5 feet long and mounted horizontally was razor sharp.

This machine was pulled around by the jeep at about 10-15 mph. The chief operated the cutter and there was a box which picked up the snow that's scraped off. The box is a V-shaped contraption built of very heavy lumber and steel which holds it together. A cable on the front couples it to the back of the cutter and a rope from the back where the V comes together is what the box man controls it with. Al Erber was the box man and his job was to hold the rope so the box didn't slide all over the place and to lift it up from the back end so that the snow was left behind at the pit. Of course, the box weighed over 200 lbs and so does Al.

After the jeep had gone around 7 times, the chief stopped and came over to where Greg, Chino and I were sitting on the rail holding our pans. "Ok, Brown, Johnson and Chino, here's what I want you to do. You see all that loose snow that's lying close to the rail and some that fell out of the box? I want you to skate around and pan up all that snow and push it over to where the box can pick it up. Now, I don't want to look around and see one guy panning his ass off and the other two sitting on the rail." After the chief got started we proceeded with our clean-up job.

Greg was a very happy-go-lucky type of guy. He was eighteen and lived at home with his mother and grandmother and he said he was going to take his first pay check and pay down on a Honda. Chino was twenty-two and an art student and he also did a job touching up paintings for some museum, plus he was a lady's man, whatever that was. Lee Taylor, who was working the squeegee on the box just now, was a carpenter plus he made belts on the side, but as there were no carpenter jobs, he would work here for the winter. Mike Chernov was some kind of intellectual even though he was very quiet and kept to himself most of the time. The chief, Walter Shumway was a judo expert and tomorrow after work, he was going for his black belt. The skinny kid who went with me to the Arsenal was Joe Squirmie, who now was driving the tractor which had a snow plow mounted on the front. His job was to push the snow away before the jeep came around to pass the pit again. Jim Clifford skated alongside the snow plow with a pan holding in the snow so that the plow didn't lose it all before it got to the pit. The jeep went around in a circle until the circle became smaller and smaller and there was only a little spot left.

After we were all finished, we had about half an hour left before the session started at 2:30 p.m. Meanwhile, the afternoon crowd was being let in and many of them were starting to go on the ice. Walter had us to put on our full uniforms and go on the ice to keep them off before 2:30. In the meantime, George made an announcement on the PA system to the effect that "This session starts at 2:30. Anyone found on the ice before that time will be put out without a refund. Please do not go on the ice."

There was a large group of people on the Deck, as it is called, because it's above the level of the ice rink. There were curiosity seekers, tourists taking pictures and people who simply wanted to skate but didn't want to wait on line. As it was almost 2:30, George went on the PA system again. "May I have your attention please, during this session the following rules and regulations will be observed: While on the skating surface you must keep moving at all times. Don't stop to congregate and carry on unnecessary conversation. When you're tired leave the ice and sit down to rest. Don't skate against traffic. Don't sit on or climb over the railing. You aren't allowed to eat or drink while on the ice. Don't smoke while on the ice. Please confine all figure skating to the center of the rink. Please cooperate with the guards and obey these rules. When you hear the music, you may skate." At the sound of the music everybody was off the boardwalk and onto the ice in a mad dash of screaming, laughing, skating and falling down.

I got busy chasing people off the rail and picking up little kids from the ice, when I noticed that there were a lot of nice girls on the ice. Most of my fellow skate guards were talking to them.

At about 3:15 p.m., George made another announcement and by this time the night crew began to come on and the day crew began to leave. I went into the locker room and to my surprise nobody was going home. Everybody was changing into their regular clothes and putting their skates back on and going back onto the ice. Greg and Al were sitting lacing on their skates. Al wondered if I was going home. "Hey, Marvelous Marv, you ain't going home yet, are you?" "Yeah, Ace," said Greg. "Stick around a while, you might go back out there and catch something nice." "Yeah, Marvelous," said Al or something nice might catch you . . . if you don't skate too fast." I was still surprised and I said, "But the supervisor said no fraternizing . . ." Greg, looked up, "Who, Cyclops? Aw, he's gone home already." "Oh he is" "Yeah, man he's sitting somewhere out on Long Island drinking martinis by now. He ain't even thinking about you." They both laughed at me and left the locker room. I put my skates on again, even though my feet were killing me and I was very tired. I skated around once before I saw Greg and Al, who weren't skating with any girls at all but were skating with each other. "Hey Marvelous, I see you hung around." "Oh Yeah, I'm checking them out," I replied. Just then, a girl who was skating in front of me, fell and I stopped to help her up. "Oh, thank you. You're very kind." "Don't mention it" I said. "I do it out of habit." "What do you mean?" she asked. "I work here." "Oh well, that's different," she said, looking very disappointed. "Where do you work?" I asked. "I work for the phone company," she answered. "My name is Marvin." I told her. "Oh, I'm Connie." She stopped and looked, searchingly through the crowd, as though expecting someone. "Oh, I wonder what happened to Michael"

"Who?" I asked. "My little brother she said, that's why I'm here. Oh, here he comes now."

"Hi Connie," a chubby little fellow skated past, though not so steady on his feet. He was working rather hard to keep up with another kid he was skating with. "He kept begging me to take him ice-skating, so finally I gave in. But it's so far down here and it takes so long on the subway." "Where do you live?" I asked. "Oh, I live way up in the Bronx, 174th at the corner of Crotona Park." "Do you always give in?" "Oh, I'll do anything for Michael," she said. "Do you and Michael live alone?' "Oh, no, we live with our parents, but they're moving pretty soon though." "Are you going to live alone after that?" "Oh no, it's just that we don't live in such a good neighborhood. Last week, someone took my mother's handbag at the subway station. She doesn't like that station," she said. I was trying to keep the conversation about her personally, but she didn't seem to catch on and she kept talking nervously about something else. "I don't like riding the subway either," she went on. I interrupted her and said, "How old are you, if you don't mind me asking?" "Why don't I look nineteen?" "Oh, yeah indeed," I replied before I realized what I should say. "I mean, I was just curious, I actually thought you were around twenty-two." "Oh, do I really look that old?" Just when I thought that I had blown it, she said, "Thank you! I'm delighted to hear someone say I look older instead of younger."

Just then, Al Erber and Greg Johnson zipped past in a zigzag pattern that you can only do when you're wearing hockey-skates. "Look out there Marvelous." "What's happening, Ace?" I did find Connie rather interesting. Even though she was just a tiny bit plump for her height, and she wore her hair up in a bun like an old school teacher. However, I was too tired at this point to do much about it. With all the excitement of the first day on the job compared to all the other jobs that I had, over the past years, this wasn't like a job at all. There was actually only about three hours of physical manual labor during the eight hours that I was there. But then, it was still only the first day.

It was now 5:00 p.m. and the crowd had gotten noticeably smaller. Connie had stumbled and almost fallen. I caught her hand as she reached out and after she regained her balance, she just sort of held on to my hand. Just then the music stopped and someone was mumbling my name, not very clear but understandable. "Brown, come into my office! Skate guard Brown come into the office!" I came to a stop and asked Connie if she was coming down tomorrow. She replied, "Oh . . . oh sure Marv. I'll see if I can leave Michael home." "Ok, I'll see you," I told her. "Ok Marv and thanks for helping me." I skated off and went into the office. The red-haired woman, who I knew as Carmela, sitting behind her desk said, "Here he is now."

A little short man looked to be about fifty and wearing a Park foreman's uniform, had been standing on top of the radiator looking out the window toward the back of the rink. He jumped down and came forward. "Brown, Are you Marv Brown?" Carmela answered before I could say anything. "Yes that's him!" The man spoke, "Brown, you forgot to sign out. All you new guys never sign out. I always got to keep reminding you guys to sign out. Your chief is supposed to see that you guys sign out, and there's two other guys down here who didn't sign out." He picked up the blotter to have a closer look and said, "Erber and Johnson didn't sign out." I said, "They're out on the ice right now." He said, "Go tell 'em both I want to see 'em." I turned and started out. "Brown," I stopped, "Sign out Brown . . . What's the matter with you guys?" I signed out. As I started out toward the exit, Al and Greg skated off. I informed them that the foreman wanted to see them and Greg said to Al, "Who's the foreman today?" "Dominick," said Al. "Oh" said Greg "OINK OINK, wants to squeal to us." Greg leaned back against the railing and looked up toward the deck where there was a group of girls standing and looking down.

Greg started to sing, "Oh squeal to me, squeal to me, squeal to me . . . ." The girls all blushed and went away. "Hey Marvelous, what happened to that nice girl I just saw you with?" asked Al. "Oh, she has probably left by now," I said. "Yeah," said Al. I just saw her getting into a chauffeured Rolls Royce." "Oh really," I said with surprise. "Aw, don't listen to him," said Greg as he waved Al off. "He's pulling your leg. Actually, it was a Cadillac she got into . . ." They both laughed at the expression on my face. Just then, the window opened and the foreman leaned out and yelled for Greg Johnson and Al Erber. When I was leaving, they were still being lectured on signing out.

On my way home I fell asleep on the subway and had it not been for some old lady sitting next to me and poking me in the ribs with her elbow, I would have ridden past my stop. Because my head was bowed a little too far in her direction, she mumbled something about people having one too many. I lived in Brooklyn and as soon as I got home, I turned on the news. I decided to lie across the bed for a few minutes before I cooked something to eat. It was 8 o'clock.

I lay down for a minute and must have fallen asleep because the next thing I knew, I had a terrible cramp in my right leg. I jumped up and stretched my leg out and had to stand that way for a moment. Meanwhile, it seemed as though I had a million muscles in my body and each one protesting every movement I made. The clock said 1:30 a.m. I decided I was too sore to cook and eat so I turned off the light and got back in the bed. I didn't sleep too well the rest of the night. The cramps in my legs kept me awake on and off. At 5:30 a.m., I was up before the sun. I washed up and dressed and was on my merry way. It was Sunday today and I had been told to be in at 7:30 a.m. as there was a special figure and dance session this morning, starting at 9 o'clock. The ice had to be specially done. I got off the train at Columbus Circle. It was fifteen to seven. It was starting out to be a nice day.

The sun was shining through the trees, which were in the process of shedding their leaves. I decided to walk the park drive down to the rink, as the park was closed to vehicles until later in the day. A group of bike riders would peddle past me every now and then, scattering pigeons and sending squirrels off to their respective hiding places. As I came down the hill to the rink, I saw the chief skating slowly over the ice and looking down as if he was searching for something. As I approached the office, he skated off and said, "Morning Brown." "Hi Walt," I spoke, signed in and went into the locker room. Most of the crew seemed to be there and ready to go. When I walked in, it sounded like everybody spoke at once, "There he is, "Marvelous my boy, what's happening Ace, "Hi yah fella." I got into my skates and the chief came in and started to talk. "Alright, now here's what we're going to do. There is a very light frost on the ice this morning, but I don't think we'll have to pan it so what we'll do is spray and squeegee and spray. Everyone ready, let's pull out the hose." As we started out, Joe Squirmie asked, "What are we going to do Walt?" Upon hearing this question, the chief got very angry and spoke very rapidly in a loud tone of voice.

"Dammit Joe, you ask the same dumb question everyday you're here and every time we do the ice. I just finished . . . where the hell were you, when I was talking? Every session it's the same thing, you never know what you're going to do before you get there. And during the session you're more trouble than you're worth. I'll tell you what we're going to do. You're going to move that hose around and I don't want to see no lines melted into that ice, and after you've finished that, you're going to get the shovel and go to the pit . . . did you understand that? Alright let's get that hose out."

Joe Squirmie didn't answer. He just stood looking helpless and lost. The hose is kept on a reel inside the window at the opposite end of the building from where our locker room was. To pull it out, one guy takes the nozzle end of it and everybody else follows with the hose over their shoulders, about ten feet behind each other, leaning forward and pulling hard. Under the strain and weight, we looked like a team of Egyptian slaves out of "The Ten Commandments," pulling up the capstone for The Great Pyramid. We got our squeegees and got very busy. Squirmie was hopping around trying to keep the hose from burning a hole in the ice. After we finished and got the hose rolled up, the chief said, "We'll go up for breakfast."

He picked two guys from the blotter to watch the figure and dance session. The two guys last to sign-in always got the job. Squirmie finished taking off his skates and asked the chief very politely, "Do I go to breakfast, Walt?" Upon hearing this, the chief shouted, "Get a shovel and get over to the pit. The concession opens at 10 o'clock. You can eat then!!!" We left as Papa Joe was making the lines to form the special patches for figure and dance and free style skating. As I hadn't eaten dinner at home the night before, my stomach was really shaking hands with my backbone. I really drew some attention when I ordered a double order of pancakes, double order of bacon, a large bowl of oatmeal and two cups of coffee. After an hour, we returned to the rink and changed into our uniforms and skates.

The chief told us to pick up the yellow cones which are normally placed in two lines across the ice on Sunday mornings to help skaters recognize the boundaries within which they may perform their respective figure eights or dancing or whatever type of trick skating that strikes their particular fancies. After we removed the cones, the chief came on the PA system. "May I have your attention please. The figure and dance session is now over. Everyone will please skate in a counter clock-wise direction around the rink. Please confine all figure skating to the center of the rink. There's no spinning or jumping permitted. Please don't sit on or climb over the railing. There's absolutely no speed skating permitted, anyone found speed skating will be asked to leave. You aren't allowed to carry food, drinks or cigarettes onto the ice. Don't throw candy or gum wrappers onto the ice surface. Please cooperate with us and obey the rules!" The long line of people who had been waiting outside the door was half inside the building by now. The chief came out and instructed half of us to go to lunch from eleven to twelve and half to go from twelve to one, including Joe Squirmie who was to continue in the pit until eleven, go to lunch and then skate from twelve to one. The chief then went into the coffee shop where he stood in front of the large window drinking coffee and talking to a very pretty girl while keeping an eye on us. The girl was one of the figure and dance instructors working for Van Gassner. Her name was Anne.

The Sunday morning crowd was generally made up of doctors, lawyers and other types of professional people. About half of the crowd was under 30. I had gone around a few times but decided that I had best take it easy or I might wind up having cramps again and be unable to sleep. Little did I know that I wasn't going to be doing much sleeping anyway. Greg was standing in the back of the rink with his arms folded across his chest and looking rather serious, so I decided to stop skating and stand next to him. I inquired if there was something wrong and he looked very surprised as he answered, "Wrong? No Ace, what makes you think that?" "Well" I said, "You look very serious right now and I know you are usually a very happy-go-lucky type." "Well, let me tell you something Ace, you see those three guys coming around the turn on speed skates?"

He pointed to three heavy set guys in their early 20's. I indicated that I saw them. "Well they are bigger than me and every now and then, I have to yell at them to slow down. So I give 'em the meanest look I got. Maybe they won't give me no lip!" "Oh, I see," I said. After that, he told me about his job in the summer as a life guard at the John Jay swimming pool, located in a fancy rich neighborhood on East 78th street. Then someone came on the PA system and said, "Skate guards at the back of the rink, too much blue." "Let's go Ace. That's our cue," said Greg as he dropped his arms and skated away. I followed a little bewildered. I asked him, "What does he mean too much blue?"

"Well, Old Cyclops stands on the top of the radiator in the office and takes a hat count to see how many skate guards are on the ice" So what you got to do is take your hat off whenever you're doing something you're not supposed to be doing, such as, two guards standing in one spot. This way he can't see you." So I asked him. "Why don't you just go over and tell him what you're trying to do?" Greg laughed as he said, "Aw, he wouldn't believe that. He'd just think I was trying to pull his beard." Suddenly, Al Erber was blowing his whistle and holding both arms up over his head which was the signal for a stretcher. Greg went for the stretcher which is kept standing at the front of the garage. I and the other guards, as well as almost all of the skaters converged on the spot where Al was still frantically blowing his whistle. I started blowing my whistle to get through the crowd and tried to keep them moving. I finally got through the crowd to where Al was standing. There was a young woman lying on the ice. Al had placed his hat under her head so she didn't have to lie with her head in contact with the ice while she waited for the stretcher.

Greg came and we carried her off, into the first aid room. She had caught her foot between the ice and the bottom of the rail, where there is an open space for draining water from the ice. She had sprained her ankle and I guess it must have really hurt because she was crying like a baby. The ambulance came and took her to Roosevelt Hospital. Four guys including myself had a fifteen minute break after which we skated until 12 o'clock and went to lunch. No one seemed to be very hungry as they all sat around and took turns playing chess. I had never learned to play the game myself, so I sat around and watched too. But from what I could see, it didn't make much sense. The intellectual was having a game with the chief and they didn't seem to move the pieces too often. Finally, Chernov moved his queen and called check mate. The chief sighed and stood up and stretched himself and said. "I'll beat you yet, Mike!" It was fifteen minutes before 1 o'clock, so George went out to make an announcement. The chief told us to be ready to go on the ice in 5 minutes and help the rest of the guys to get the people off. George was talking on the PA system, May I have your attention please:

"This session ends in fifteen minutes in order to avoid congestion at the checkout counter we advise you to start checking out now. Thank you." At one o'clock George was on the PA system, "May I have your attention please. This session is now over. Will every one please leave the ice. Leave the ice at the nearest exit. Turn in your rental skates and claim your checked articles. Thank you and come back again."

Most of the crowd went into the building in a congested mass. However, there were a few others on the ice trying to go one more time around. An incident occurred between Joe Squirmie and a man who Joe thought wasn't leaving the ice fast enough.

The man couldn't skate too well, and tried to make his way to the rail and then to the exit. Anyway, Joe pushed the man before he could get to the rail. The man fell to the ice and when he got up, his nose was bleeding and he was very angry and started to yell for the police.

The supervisor who was standing just in front of the office was looking on and came running out on the ice, "What's going on here?" he yelled. The man who was very excited said, "I want the police, I'm having this guard arrested?" The supervisor explained that he had observed what happened and that he was sorry, and asked that the man not press charges against Squirmie and that he would fire him on the spot right now, instead. The man agreed and Joe was told to turn in his uniform. The crowd for the afternoon session had already formed a line that looked to me like it was ten deep and half way round the park. We went out and reconditioned the ice. The rest of the crew was talking about Squirmie's incident, and Greg said, "Just as well, he wasn't wrapped too tightly in the brain anyway."

By the time we finished the ice, half the line was in and by 2:30 there were so many people around the boardwalk and inside the building that there wasn't room enough to move around. The afternoon session started and people really packed themselves onto the ice so well that there wasn't enough room to fall down. Al Erber skated past me. "Look out now Marvelous, there's some nice ones out here today," meaning the girls. He was gone before I could say anything but I had to admit, I was just like a kid in a candy store. There were still a lot of people who didn't get into the building as they don't like to let more than three thousand in, because it's harder to control the crowd, especially as the afternoon, weekend and holidays are made up of teenage school kids. Of course, there are a dozen cops from the special events squad assigned to the rink on weekends and holidays, and a couple of cops from The Central Park Precinct are assigned at all other times.

Today, these cops were posted in various places around the rink and along the fence to stop anyone from climbing over. I was busy as usual, trying to keep people from rubbing the paint off that precious rail and yelling at speed skaters who seemed to be hell bent on violating the speed rules. Suddenly, a familiar voice said, "Hi Marv!" I did a fast stop and about face and to my surprise, there was that girl from yesterday's afternoon session. "Hi" I greeted her. I had to sneak away from home while Michael was out. I had to give him a dollar and send him to the pizza shop with his friend. He loves pizza!" She laughed nervously and continued, "and then, I got down here and almost didn't get in. Such a crowd! Would you believe I was the last one they let in?" "Really" I said.

"I didn't know exactly what to say to her as I was surprised to see her and had forgotten that she was supposed to come by today, but I couldn't tell her that. "Well yes," I said. "It's quite crowded today and that's why they only let in so many and stop the line. "Yah know something? "What?" "This is a nice job you have." "You think so?" "Oh, sure. I mean all you do is skate around, and every now and then you tell someone to get off the rails or something like that. I don't think it's hard at all." "Well I'm not supposed to be skating for pleasure. I'm supposed to at least look like I'm working, even if I'm not." "There's a guy who isn't doing anything . . . ," she pointed toward the pit as we were coming around and there was Al Erber doing chop sticks on the skates. Connie asked, "What is he doing anyway?" "Chop sticks." "Chop sticks." "Yeah that's right!" "What's he doing that for Marv?" "Oh, he's just clowning around." "Yes, but doesn't he mess up the ice when he does that?" "Probably, but never mind him, let's talk about you!" "Me . . . . Oh, what do you want to know about me?" For instance, what do you plan to do after this session?" "Oh, I don't know. Actually, I hadn't planned to do anything." "Why?" She looked up at me and smiled. "Well," I said, "Why don't we get together for a while?" "Sure Marv, why not?"

About this time, some of the night crew began to skate past and I realized it was quitting time. I told Connie to go in and take off her skates and wait for me in front of the garage. I went and started to change into my street clothes. The rest of the crew was doing the same and many had already left. Al and Greg came in. "Marvelous, I see you're doing all right for yourself.

Yeah Ace, you're doing better than what we're doing. "Is that a fact," I said with a broad grin. "I think I'd better get cracking boys, cause there's something nice waiting for me out there. Thanks fellas!" "Thanks," said Greg and Al looking at each other. "What for Ace?" "Well, it was you guys who told me to stick around, remember." I left the locker room and when I got to the front of the garage, Connie was waiting for me. She had her skates with her so I took them and put them in my locker so that we wouldn't have to carry them around. We then left the rink and walked out to 6th Avenue and 59th Street, and from 59th Street to Columbus Circle.

"Where are we going Marv," asked Connie. "Would you like to go to a movie?" I asked. "Sure why not. What are we going to see?" "Well lets us see. I think there is something playing out in Brooklyn that I would like to see." "Ok Marv, whatever you say." And those were the words I wanted to hear and off we went to Brooklyn.

Once in Brooklyn, I decided the picture they're showing wasn't what I wanted to see. I suggested we go to my house and listen to a little music on my stereo set. She agreed and soon we're at my house and I was cooking smoked sausage and grits and making toast for the two of us. The setting was perfect as Mama Sara wasn't going to be home that day. We ate and drank coke. Afterward, we sat on my bed and had a bottle of wine, while I told her my life's story and listened to the tape recorder. "Gee, Marvin that was a very good dinner." "Thank you!" I said. "But who taught you to cook like that?" "My grandmother," I said. "Oh boy, I don't know any guys that can really cook and I never ate anything like that before. What was that anyway?" "Oh, it was just some grits and smoked hot pork sausage." "Boy, it sure was good. We never cooked anything like that at my house." Oh really, what do you all cook?" "Oh we just eat bacon and eggs for breakfast and some kind of canned stuff for dinner. Sometimes my mother makes a ham." "Well, how about that" I said. I kissed her once, twice and three times and I don't exactly remember just what happened after that. "I never met anyone like you before." "Well I'll tell you, there isn't anybody like me but me and when I'm gone, there'll be no more." Then she laughed her nervous laugh.

We made our way up to the subway. Only thing is that at 1:00 a.m., the Transit Authority seemed to be on vacation. The train finally came and we rode half asleep all the way up to the Bronx, 174th Street. I saw her to her door and started on my way back. At this time in the morning, the subways are loaded with drunks, transvestites, rowdies and junkies. I was glad to get to Eastern Parkway. It had been three hours since I left home and I was glad to be home again. It was now 4:00 a.m. I undressed and fell into bed. I was asleep for what seemed an unbelievably short time. The alarm clock went off at 6:00 a.m. and I went off at 7:00 a.m. Half walking and half crawling with my eyes half closed, I managed to find my way to the subway, and was even lucky enough to find a seat. Good thing too, because I think I would have had trouble standing and sleeping at the same time. I walked into the locker room and it looked like everyone was there except Al Erber and George Finlayson who was off today. "Morning Ace, boy whatever happened to you," said Greg. "Your eyes look like the New York State road map. Has somebody been pulling you through the mill or something?" Before I could figure out what to say, the chief spoke, "Brown, I don't know boy, you look like something's been dragging you all over the park." "Yep, that pretty much sums it up!" I replied. Did I really look that bad? On my way out to the ice, I went to the men's room and took a look in the mirror. Two baggie red eyes stared back at me, plus I hadn't combed my hair and I forgot to wear my hat.

While we were doing the ice, Greg asked, "Say, didn't I see you leaving here yesterday with a girl? Yeah, I think it was you, only I saw you from the back as you were going over the hill toward 6th Avenue. I knew you were skating with her during the session." I acknowledged that it was me, after which Greg laughed and said, "Oh, so that's why you look so dead. You've been out all night having a ball!" "No, no," I said. You got it all wrong. The ball was having me!" "My man's fast with the lips and fast with the hips!" said Chino.

After we rolled up the hose, everybody went up for breakfast except me. I lay down on one of the benches in the locker room and I drifted off to sleep. While hanging onto the outskirts of never, never land, I could faintly discern some kind of commotion in the immediate vicinity. Someone said, "Check Mate" and somebody else complained about somebody else not minding their own business and stop telling someone which moves to make and to let him win or lose the game by himself. Anyway, somebody tried to pull me off the bench as they said, "Wake up, Ace and get your uniform and skates on. I sat up and there was Greg dressed and ready to go, along with everybody else.

TRIBUTE TO A SKATE GUARD

When the ice you make is lousy,
But you've done the best you can,
And von Gassner's ice instructors,
Just refuse to understand.
When you find the hose has frozen,
And the pit is full of snow,
The night crew broke the jeep,
Too bad the night before.
When the box you box is heavy,
And the pit so far away,
The driver must think he's running,
In a race on Labor Day.
When the bosses are all against you,
And all the public too,
They find fault with your skating,
And other work you do.
When Hollywood's on location,
And you're left out of the film,
Bob takes all the money,
And your future's looking dim,
As long as Rickie brings your pay check,
And your best girl loves you true,
Just stand tall and proud on your silver, red and blue.

Marvin Brown with the ice crew 1972

CHAPTER II

It was really a nice day today. The sun was shining and it was around 35 degrees cold. The music started and the small crowd of old ladies and old men were off to a merry start. Most of them skated arm in arm or hand in hand or they did some kind of fancy dance spinning and twirling and gliding little powder puff ballerinas in a Walt Disney cartoon. Only thing is nobody seemed to regard the rules about confining all figure and dance to the center of the rink. So, I felt compelled to do my duty and speak to a few of these happily dancing people on this matter. One old lady in particular was quite annoyed at me, so she went over to Mr. Viola, who happened to be the foreman for the day, and complained." That red-eyed skate guard is continuously and unnecessarily harassing me." The foreman told her, "Yes madam, I have been observing your skating myself and I noticed you're dancing all over the track. You're to confine your figure skating to the center of the rink and none of this: The foreman, his cigar in his right hand which he held up over his head and tipped up on one foot as if to imitate a skater spinning. His cigar ashes fell off the top of his hat. And none of that: He leaned forward on one foot and with his other foot stretched out behind him and with both arms out stretched like the wings of an airplane and his head back, he imitated a skater gliding on one foot. And none of this: He then put his hand on his hip and tipped up on one foot and spun around and hopped backwards catching himself on one foot, imitating a skater jumping. And madam, if you persist on breaking the rules, I'll have no other choice but to ask you to leave the premises". That poor woman looked thoroughly shocked as she left in a huff, as she exclaimed, "I'm going to write a letter to the Commissioner of Parks." Mr. Viola winked at me, smiled and went into the office to make an announcement concerning the rules and regulations.

The chief had been leaning against the garage all the time talking to that pretty instructor, whistled to get my attention and to call me over to talk to me. "Yah know Brown, you don't have to push those rules too hard during weekdays. After all there's only a handful here most of the week. All these old people you see out here now, have been coming here six days a week for every season as far back as I can remember and they still can't skate to save their life. Anyway, if you guys speak to somebody out there for doing something wrong, the boss has to back you up. I mean that's what he got you out there for in the first place." I nodded a coupled of times to let him know I understood as he continued to speak, "Kate Wollman's family put up the money to build this place for the kids, but these people come here everyday from Park Avenue and act like this place belongs to them personally. I'm sick of looking at them myself." I was told to take a fifteen minute break and to take Greg with me. Just then another old woman came off to complain that a skate guard, she pointed to Greg, had skated past her too fast and that he frightened her so that she fell down. Greg and I went into the coffee shop as he complained, "That old lady does nothing but make us miserable every time she comes down here. I mean I didn't even go near her, she fell all by herself. The next time she falls in front of me, I'm going to do a figure eight on her kidneys." I nodded my agreement and approval and told him not to get too excited about it. I could see he was angry after being made the scapegoat for somebody's inability to skate.

He continued to let off steam. "I know they don't think much of skate guards. They think a skate guard is just some low form of life that was hatched under a rock somewhere out in the park, after which his existence is barely tolerated on the ice at Wollman Rink where he's supposed to be seen and not heard. Well, I got just two words for them and it sure ain't Merry Christmas." Frank Doolittle was on the other side of the coffee counter fixing the coffee. He fixed us a couple of coffees and asked how the job was going. "Well," said Greg, "aside from some old bag trying to give me a hard time, everything's cool!" Frank leaned forward over the counter and started talking. "You know I have to change some spotlights pretty soon and I was wondering if . . . ." "Come on Ace, let's get out of here," said Greg. "Otherwise this guy is going to have us doing our job and his too." "Does he work in the restaurant too?"

"Hell, no, he doesn't work at all! He just finds some excuse to hang out behind the counter. This way he can drink up all the coffee and eat up all the cakes." Our break was over and we returned to the ice so that a couple of other guys could be relieved. Since we went to lunch from 12 until 1 yesterday, today we're told to go from 11 to 12. This way everyone gets a chance to have a late lunch. I was glad to be able to lie down and go to sleep for an hour more. "Well, I guess I'll go down here and let Calvin make me another one of those squirrel-burgers!" Greg said. I inquired, "What was a squirrel-burger?" "Ace, a squirrel-burger is a hamburger made from squirrels. You notice you don't see too many squirrels running around here, do you? Well that's because Calvin cooked them and the skate guards ate them all up!" Needles to say, I didn't believe a word of it, with Greg having a tendency for making jokes about everything and everybody. I figured he was just putting me on.

He went off to get his squirrel burger and I . . . well, was impatiently trying to find the most comfortable position to lay on a bench 12 inches wide. I never did get to sleep, but as I'm off tomorrow, I intend to spend the whole day trying to make up for it. After Greg and I were back on the ice, we spent some time observing some of the skaters and the way they skated. I pointed out one old man who was short with slightly rounded shoulders. He wore speed skates and the way he skated made him look a lot like a weasel. After which between ourselves, we so named him. "Oh sweat Ace, look at that," said Greg. I looked around to see what he was marveling at. "See no evil, hear no evil, speak no evil," said Greg. There were three old-aged women skating arm in arm. One wore figure skates, the second wore hockey skates and the third wore speed skates. To me they seemed quite a merry trio. "What are we going to call them Ace?" "I don't know."

"What do you want to call them?" "The one in the middle, wearing speed skates has bowed legs so we'll call her the chimpanzee lady. The one with the figure skates, built like a baboon, so we'll call her the baboon lady and the one with the hockey skates is wearing a coat with big pockets so she looks like a kangaroo, so that's what we'll call her. "Ok," I agreed. "Whatever you say." "Hey look at this guy." He pointed to a middle aged man with gray hair who was skating with a young girl in her late teens or early twenties. He was skating with her left hand in his and his right arm around her waist as far as he could reach and then up. "Just look at him Ace. Hey, you know who that is? That's old Wolfie up to his old tricks again. He thinks he's a lady killer." "Hey look at this chick with the flat chest!" I pointed her out. Greg laughed. "Suppose we call her sunny?" She always asked why we called her that. The chimpanzee lady managed to get her speed skate blade caught in the baboon's lady's figure skates and they all went down with the kangaroo lady doing some fancy hopping in a vain effort to stay on her feet. "Look at the chest on this one Ace!" "Yeah, I'm checking it out. Boy, if she falls, she'll just bounce right up again." Greg laughed and said, "Ace, boy I swear to God, some time you break my funny bone." The session ended and we did the ice. Al was off today but he was here anyway. He had an interest in one of Von's instructors, a shapely little number named Linda. They were sitting on a bench and Al was lacing up her skates as they planned to skate for a while.

Greg and I weren't standing far away. The chief came over with the drill and pad and told Greg and me to take soundings. Greg was talking to Al. "Boy, I swear, on a sailor's day off, he goes on a boat ride. On a mail man's day off, he takes a walk in the park, and on a skate guard's day off he goes skating at Wollman Rink. "What the hell's the matter with you Al?" Al looked up from what he was doing. "Why don't you get out on that ice and take soundings, like Walter told you." "Yeah, I know, said Greg, you just can't get Wollman out of your blood." "Yeah, but you're half right, it's not, Wollman that I have in my blood. Linda smiled and rubbed her nose against Al's cheek. "Ok Ace, said Greg to me. "How do you want to do this? Do you want to drill while I write, or do you want me to write while you drill?" I didn't quite catch what he meant. "Watch it Marvelous," said Al. "Sounds like he's trying to get slick on yah! Give him the drill and let him drill all 99 of them holes."

I decided that I would drill half and Greg the other half, with me first. As we worked, little kids would come over and ask, "What are you making holes in the ice for?" To which Greg would answer, "We're making holes in the ice so the fish can breathe." "Is there fish down there for real?" "Sure there is! Show her the fish Ace." I took away the drill and the little girl got on her knees and put her nose against the ice in an effort to see through the hole. "There ain't no fish down there!" "Sure there is, but they're all invisible!" "Well, I've never seen an invisible fish before." "That's probably why you can't see them." At that time, the little girl's mother came over. "Wendy, what on earth . . . come away dear, the men are measuring the ice." Wendy left protesting and insisted on having another look at the invisible fish. Another kid came over and the whole thing started all over again. Pretty soon some of the night crew started to go past. Greg was more anxious than I was to leave the ice.

"Come on Ace, let's go in the locker room." I asked him if he thought it possible to teach me chop-sticks. "Well, Marvelous, the thing you gotta do is go down to Jessie Halpern's skate shop and let old Bernie fix you up with a pair of hockey skates. A good pair of Bauer's should do. After you've done that, then, come talk to me. Yeah Ace, I'll teach you everything you want to learn," said Greg. "No you don't Marvelous. If you want to learn the correct way, don't let him teach you!" Tomorrow, Tuesday was my day off, and I'd planned to sleep from dawn to dawn. I emerged from my house Wednesday morning under a massive down-pour of rain. By the time I arrived at work, it had let up and the supervisor told the chief it would be a good idea to squeegee off the ice before it started raining again. We all went out and interlocked our squeegees together and pushed the largest puddles off. Just as we finished, the rain started again. We returned to the locker room and for the rest of the day. Everyone just sat around playing cards or playing chess or sleeping. At one point the chess set was unoccupied so Greg was trying to teach me the moves. After I thought I understood, he set up the board and we started to play a game. He had the lighter pieces and after about four moves he said, "Ok Ace, you just made your last move in this game. Check Mate!"

I protested that, "The game couldn't be over that quick, especially when the chief and the intellectual play one game for as much as an hour." "Well Ace, the difference is that you have just been caught in the fools mate. What you should have done, was put your, Queen in front of your King and left it there." We played a few more games and Greg explained in more detail which moves not to make and why I shouldn't make them and with each game we played it took me longer to lose.

After two weeks on the job, we received our first paycheck and I went into Bernie and spent $48.00 on a pair of hockey skates, laced them on and took to the ice and spent a lot of time on my knees trying to stand up. It was unbelievable that after skating for four years on a pair of speed skates that I paid $20 for, I was unable to stand up wearing a brand new pair of $50 hockey skates.

It was a good thing Al was on the ice and gave me a few tips on how to stand up and skate. And it was a good thing that it was after work. Otherwise, I would have surely disgraced my uniform. "The trick, Marvelous, is to lean back." On speed skates the weight is mostly on the front of the blade but on hockey, the weight is on the back. I was soon able to stand up and skate without rocking and bowing like a motor boat. I wanted to learn to do a ring turn. "Now what you gotta do Marvelous, is pull your left knee back, as you ride the inside edge on your right skate." I wanted to learn the tee stop also. Al gladly obliged. By Sunday morning, I was zipping around that ice like somebody from the New York Rangers. Oh, sweet happy days, you're here at last. And before the session was over, I managed to incur quite a bit of displeasure from a rather conservative Sunday morning crowd and somebody stopped me and said, "You really know how to whip around out here, don't you."

After that the boss called me in and chewed on my ears a while. After spending much of the week-end with Connie, I was on my way into work Monday morning and somebody yelled "Get out of the road Ace, before you get run over!" Whatever it was, buzzed on past me like an angry bumble bee and went tearing off down the drive in the direction of the rink. I soon learned it was only a mad skate guard on a motorcycle. By the time I reached the rink, the whole crew was upstairs admiring Greg's new Honda. Greg was sitting on it and proudly exhibiting and demonstrating all the gadgets and gimmicks on the handle bars. It was black and silver and had 160cc whatever that was. The boss managed to get our attention and let us know that the ice not only still existed, but needed lots of tender love and care. We got on with the job and as we worked, I noticed a rather well dressed man standing around in a supervisor's uniform. He wore eye glasses and had dark hair. His name was Mr. Joe Defazio and I heard someone say he was to be the new supervisor.

Ginkilla was being promoted to Assistant Borough Director of Queens. It was said that Ginkilla had been supervisor at the rink for 15 years, from the day they opened the place in 1950. He had tried many times to move up but it seemed that his superiors in the upper part of the Arsenal kept pushing him back down, because they didn't want him jumping on their gravy train. However, old Ginkilla never passed up an opportunity to make trouble for them and generally kept them uncomfortable. Especially, since he felt that they all held their positions illegally by being politically appointed, while he was always forced to take the necessary qualification tests, which was a much slower process for getting to the top. However, he was finally moving a little higher up the ladder. Well anyway, Ginkilla was going to break in this new supervisor for a week. It didn't take the new man long to catch on, especially since he had just come from city building out in Flushing Meadows where the World's Fair was taking place. The crew called the new supervisor Joe Dee. He started out as an Assistant Gardner over in Hecksher section of the park, which is the section adjoining the Wollman section. He also studied law at night. It was said that he scored 100 on every city examination he ever took and at 28 years old, he was now the youngest General Foreman in the Department. And now he's down here as a supervisor and Doolittle will have some dues to pay. The new boss was very ambitious and started his era by ordering the keeper of the inventory to make out file cards for each skate guard which would be used to record any points against the skate guard and record any disciplinary measures taken.

He had Frank Doolittle rearrange the cable on the box so that the overflow of snow would fall on the inside of the circle instead of on the outside of the newly finished surface. He also had Frank Doolittle build a giant squeegee from police barriers which was designed to mount on to the snow plow. This was supposed to be used on a rainy day when there were extremely large puddles on the ice. It would have worked perfectly, if the cement slab onto which the ice adhered to had been level instead of high in the middle and low on both sides. This caused a hill over the ice which was more noticeable at the front and rear of the ice. This caused many skaters who, not being aware of this condition, to lose their balance and fall always in the same place. The slab, I'm told, was built over what was at one time part of the 59th Street Lake which has, since the construction of the rink, continued to settle. There has been talk of ripping the whole thing up and building it over again. Especially as some of the refrigeration lines under the cement had gone bad and didn't hold on a warm day. However, nothing ever materialized from this talk. The problem seemed to have something to do with lack of money in the budget. Frank Dolittle was griping about "all these unnecessary things" he was being forced to do. He mumbled something about the equipment that was normally constructed by the shops or ordered through the purchase department was now his responsibility. In any case, his hammer and screwdriver were really earning their keep.

Greg explained to me that he convinced his mother how badly he needed the bike to get to work and back. She gave him the money to buy it, but he had to pay her back before the end of the season. He also said that Lee Taylor taught him how to ride, which wasn't too easy as he had no conception of standard shifting. We finished for the day and were on our way out of the building when Greg said, "Hop on Ace, I'll give you a lift to the subway". "Oh no," I said. "You'll never get me on that thing!" I didn't know at that time that I would buy a motorcycle several months later.

Christmas was coming up soon and as skate guards, we aren't allowed off on weekends and holidays. During Ginkilla's time, half the crew was allowed off on New Year's Day. Mr. Joe Dee put an end to that, and needless to say, he wasn't too popular in the locker room. Especially with all of his new innovations such as keeping us out in the rain to squeegee the whole time it was raining or making us pan while it was snowing or sending us out in the park to rake leaves. On the other hand, being popular wasn't part of his job, so long as we did what he told us to do, he didn't care if we liked him or not. Plus, he didn't allow us in the office anymore, only to pick up our paychecks. He said something about over-familiarity. Frank Doolittle said, "Aw, he'll be different after he goes off to Chicago and gets married." The big snow finally came in January.

We were half-way through the season. We had all been to the Zoo Cafeteria for breakfast as the chief thought we had best get our stomachs full before we get involved with the snow. The morning session was cancelled as we would need at least half a day to try and have the ice ready for the afternoon session. The snow was deep enough to cover the top of my skates, plus it rained after the snow and there was frozen crust covering the whole thing, making it impossible to skate and necessary to walk with our skates on. After putting a fresh blade in the cutter and starting to cut close to the rail, we hooked the box onto the cutter as we came past the garage. Al had to go into the locker room to get his gloves so the chief told me to take the box until Al came back. It was my very first attempt at boxing and I guess the box was heavier than I thought because when I lifted it, my knees collapsed. The left one felt as if it had broken right off. The chief stopped the work and the boys got a stretcher and carried me off to the first aid room. George took me to Roosevelt Hospital in the jeep.

After waiting for two hours, a doctor finally came in and decided that I should be x-rayed. He couldn't find any evidence of anything wrong, so he told me to go home. Nevertheless, he gave me an appointment for the clinic for the next week. I called the rink and the boss told me to take the rest of the day off. In the meantime, I couldn't put very much weight on my left leg and took advantage of every opportunity to hold on to a banister or anything that would support me better than my left leg was doing. I went off to the subway and by the time I reached home my knee had swollen to twice its normal size and when I tried to sleep, the pain kept me up most of the night. By morning, my knee was three times its normal size. I called in sick and went to see Dr. Patterson at the clinic. He asked me a few questions about my job and the situation leading to the accident and then asked me to sit on a couch while he had a look at my knee. He held my foot in both hands and gave my leg a quick twist. Oh, Holy Moses, I jumped through the ceiling and up onto the next floor above. The pain was excruciating. The doctor did not seem at all surprised as he said, "I'm sorry Mr. Brown. I promise that I won't do that again."

CHAPTER III

Dr. Patterson was an orthopedic surgeon. He told me that I needed to have an operation to remove the damaged cartilage in my knee. I was told to report to the admitting office on the coming Sunday at 12 o'clock and that the operation would take place Monday morning. I reported to the hospital at the appointed time and was shown to a room on the 7th floor. There was an old man in the bed next to mine. I was told to undress and was given some kind of open-backed frock to put on. A doctor came in a little later to take my pulse and blood pressure. He told me I could only have juice to drink until after the operation. At 7:30 a.m. the next morning, an orderly came into our room pushing a bed with large wheels on it. He informed me that I was to climb on and he would deliver me to the operating room. I couldn't understand why I had to travel by bed since I was perfectly capable of walking since the swelling had gone down in my leg. Nevertheless, I hopped on board and felt like I was taking my last ride. My imagination was running wild.

Suppose they gave me too much anesthesia and I died or something. Suppose they made some other mistake and something else went wrong and they decided that they might as well go ahead and cut my leg off altogether. I was rolled into the operating room under a big light which was brought down to focus on my leg. Everybody was wearing Billy the Kid type masks over their faces and a nurse attached a needle to a plastic tube which was attached to a bottle of clear liquid that hung from a stand on the left side of my bed. She then shoved this very big needle into my left arm. I couldn't understand how someone so lovely could do such a cruel thing to me. I looked up to admire her and that was the last thing I remembered. For the next 3 hours I was living in limbo. A fraction of consciousness touched my brain and somewhere out in front of me was a clock moving around on a wall. Sometimes it got bigger and other times smaller or even just faded away altogether. Ah yes, I'm alive after all but just barely. Somebody said long live the skate guard.

"Ok, this one's recovered," said a voice. "Take him up to his room." The clock on the wall was still moving toward me and back to the wall again and I thought it read 11:00 or maybe it was 5 minutes to 12. It was then my turn to fade out. Once back in my room, two orderlies lifted me not too gently onto my bed and I'm sure I screamed. I wasn't sure if my leg was still there but the pain sure was. And that brought me around in a mighty big hurry. While my mind was functioning, I figured I had best feel around under the sheet and see if . . . yes all of me was still there and properly attached in their proper places. You can't trust these doctors nowadays with all the transplant operations going on. I vaguely recall someone saying something about separating the men from the . . . What smart-aleck said that? I soon faded out again. The next time I caught a glimpse of reality, there was someone in a skate guard uniform standing next to my bed and he seemed to be holding a large basket with fruit with gold colored paper covering it. "Hi, Marvin, how are you feeling?" I tried to answer but all I could do was mumble and moan.

"Brought you something from all the guys," the voice said. I guess I must have faded out again while the guy was still standing there.

The next thing I knew, it was the next morning and someone said, "Wake up and eat your breakfast. You haven't eaten for two days!" They left my tray on a bed table and went away. The bacon and eggs didn't look too appetizing and the toast looked like it had been steamed in a sauna for the past ten years. Although I'm not fussy about what I eat, I wasn't about to touch anything on that plate. The food was returned and that brought the dietician charging into see just what was the matter. A skate guard that doesn't like food is most unusual. I told her she would have to cook me some hot smoked pork sausages and grits. She probably had no idea what that was as my request was never filled. Connie came up to see me during the visiting hour later in the afternoon and I sent her out to get me a hero sandwich and king size coke. After I put away my sandwich and coke, Connie sat on the edge of the bed and was rubbing her hand over my face and saying "Oh my, Marv, poor Marv, what have they been doing to you?" Suddenly an old stone-faced nurse appeared out of nowhere and said, "Visitors aren't allowed to sit on the bed. You must sit in the chair or remain standing." She just as suddenly disappeared only to reappear again at unexpected intervals, which I thought was very impolite and unnecessary. I wonder what she expected to catch us doing.

Several days later, Connie was visiting with me when the doctor came by to take out my stitches. I asked if he was going to give me a shot in case there was some pain. He told Connie jokingly, "Take one of these crutches and hit him over the head that should deaden his pain." After Connie left, I told the nurse to bring me a TV set because I was really getting bored. The next morning some old battle axe of a nurse's aide came in and said she was going to give me a bath, but first she had to help me out of the bed so it could be changed. She started by grabbing my bad leg and trying to drag me out of the bed. I was convinced she was trying to twist my leg off at the knee. Anyway, from that date on, I was out of bed, all washed up and dressed long before she got there. Later in the day Greg came up and he had a new chess set which he bought just for me. We played a game and for the first time since he taught me how to play, I beat him. Although he looked surprised, I still think that he lost on purpose. I received a number of get well cards through the mail and one of them was from people at the rink, including all the skate guards, all the permanent staff as well as the park police. Everyone had signed his or her name, even von Gassner and his instructors. The card said, "A little something to speed up your recovery." I opened it out and it showed a nurse. Dr. Patterson came around a couple of times to see how I was doing.

They had given me a pair of crutches to walk on but after using them a few times, I decided they weren't necessary and requested a walking cane instead. The doctor was quite satisfied with my recovery and thought it remarkable that I could walk without any aid after only five days after surgery. I was told initially by the doctor that I would be in the hospital for two weeks. However, on the tenth day they threw me out. They said something about needing the bed. I had been away from work for almost three weeks. The following Monday, I returned to work. Mr. Joe Dee had me walking around the boardwalk chasing people off the rails from the outside. During conditioning, I only had to ride shotgun in the jeep. After about a week of this, I got bored and put my skates on anyway.

I never became renowned as a box man and as far as I was concerned, that box had a curse on it. The season was heading into its last lap and pretty soon it would be over and all the guys were looking forward to their summer jobs. Those who were life guards had to take a special test to re-qualify for every new season. They had been doing this since January at the 54th Street swimming pool, the life guard training center for everyone that wished to be a life guard. As for myself, I never learned to swim. In fact, I have never been in the water of a swimming pool. Of course I used to play in the creek when I was back home on the farm, but I wouldn't dare call it swimming. So, I had to figure out what I was going to do for the summer. Greg said he wasn't going to be a life guard this summer because they don't make enough money. He told me that George Finlayson recommended him to the chief engineer out at Randall's Island and he was going to work as a Filter Plant Operator (FPO) with George up at High Bridge Pool. He said that the life guards were only paid $12 a day, the same as skate guards and that an F P O's pay was $16 a day.

I inquired as to how I could get recommended and Frank Doolittle who was also in the locker room at the time heard us talking and asked me if I wanted to be a filter plant operator. I assured him that I did, after which he made a phone call to someone somewhere and gave my name, address, and phone number. He later told me that it was all fixed and that when the time came I would get a letter in the mail telling me when to report to the Arsenal. The rink closed when the season came to an end on April 15th. The pool was scheduled to open on Memorial Day weekend and we were to start work two weeks before. Meanwhile, there was a month in between the closing of the rink and the opening of the pool that we didn't have anything to do. So we were told to go over to the Arsenal and see Mary Boyle. She would fix us up with something until the pools opened. Greg and George were assigned to a park some place up in Washington Heights, not far from where they lived.

I was given a seasonal park job over at Hecksher section which is the next section over from Wollmans. I worked for a month picking up paper, dumping garbage, raking up trash, shoveling sand. I normally worked with Dave Jackson who is one of the permanent men and little Anthony who was number one man in charge while McNamara was away. Whenever I finished what I was doing, I would go to Anthony and ask, "What do you want me to do next?" At this, he was very impressed and said, "Oh boy, I've never seen a seasonal who asked what to do next. They usually just go off some place and hide." Whatever did he say that for, it started to put ideas into my head. Well, maybe it wasn't such a good idea after all. Greg came to visit me a couple of times. When McNamara, the foreman returned, it was my last day at Hecksher's and it's a good thing too, as he had a reputation for being a real terror. When he saw me he said, "I expect you to be in a Parks Dept uniform on Monday, including a green hat, shirt and pants." Fortunately, I had already been appointed to report to Sunset Pool in Brooklyn on Saturday which was the next day and I was obligated to so inform him. On Saturday, I took the subway out to Bay Ridge in Brooklyn and got off at 45th Street and found my way up to Sunset Swimming Pool. Frank Doolittle was waiting in the office for me. He introduced me to the supervisor and foreman and showed me where to sign in as F P O. We then went over to the filter house and he took me down into the filter plant to show me what it looked like. The pool itself consisted of two separate parts.

The largest part was called the swimming pool and was 3 feet deep at the lower end and the smaller section. The diving pool was 12 feet deep and was the larger section. Both parts combined held one and a half million gallons of water. "It's just a big toilet bowl," said Frank. The filter plant was situated below ground level consisted of six large tanks about 15 feet wide, 20 feet long and 40 feet deep. Five of the tanks were filled with charcoal, with two troughs in each one, and four large valves at the front of each tank. The sixth tank was called the clear well. This was the tank where the clean water from the filters accumulated. There were two electric motors on the floor that pumped the water from the clear well back into the pool. In order to get to the filters, it was necessary to climb up a ladder that was about 25 feet straight up and walk on a steel grating called a cat walk. The upper filter house was at ground level and consisted of one big room. All the chemicals were kept there, such as chlorine gas, aluminum sulfate, copper sulfate and light soda ash in 100 pound bags. These chemicals are used to treat the water.

Our job was to fill the pool with water which we were going to do on Monday and keep the water treated. The entire filter plant was a mass of giant sized pipes running in and out of tunnels and walls, with giant wheels called valves in various places, with chains hanging down. At a casual glance, it looked very confusing. Frank pointed to two islands situated in the middle of the swimming pool and said, "We have to climb inside of those islands and change all the bulbs in the under-water lights before we fill the pool." We did that on the first day and on Sunday, we did some painting in the filter house. On Monday morning, we had to change some cracked lens after the regular men had removed the covers from the under-water lights around the wall of the pool. Meanwhile, Frank was running water from a city water supply valve into the treatment tank in the filter house. The idea was to fill up all the tanks so that after all the covers had been removed from the under-water lights; we could immediately start pumping water into the pool. One of the regular men went into the filter house and when he came out, he yelled for Frank who went running. While we were working outside, all the tanks had filled up and started spilling over onto the floor of the filter plant. "Well, we're at least off to a good start," said Frank, "with the first flood of the season."

After about 16 hours from the time we started running the water, the pool was completely filled. On Tuesday, Frank showed me how to put in and connect the chlorine tanks and how to test for a chlorine leak with a bit of ammonia on a cotton swab. When the cotton swab came in contact with gas that was leaking, the two combined produced a white smoke. He showed me how to use the gas mask also. The chlorinator was the machine that mixed the gas with the water. It consisted of a large bell jar sitting on an iron table-like stand which had a top built like a four cornered trough that held about 12 inches of water. The bell jar was open at the bottom and sat in the water on top of four pins. There was left a space about 1 inch wide between the bottom of the jar and the floor of the trough to seal in the gas between the surfaces of the water on the inside of the jar.

The gas is fed into the jar through copper lines running from the chlorine cabinet into a plastic tube sticking inside of the jar. The mixture is then fed into the clear well by a jet stream of water, shooting through a hose which passes a second tube running from the bell jar. This setup creates a vacuum with so great a suction that it draws the mixture into the jet stream which introduces it into the filtered water in the clear well where it is then pumped back into the pool. The soda ash and aluminum sulfate are fed into the treatment tank where the water level is at the same level as the pool and the top of it is a little higher than ground level. These chemicals are fed from chemical feeders. The soda ash is fed 24 hours a day while the aluminum sulfate is only fed long enough to build a flock on the filters that catches the finest trash. It's then turned off. The copper sulfate is used to keep algae from growing on the walls of the pool. However, it was only used about once a week and then, only after swimming hours as this was a poisonous chemical and shouldn't be used during swimming hours.

On Tuesday, I was taught to back wash. This is the name for the process of cleaning the filters by reversing the direction of the water that normally runs into the filter from the top after closing certain valves and opening others. The water that was being pumped up through the filter brought with it dirt and filth that may have settled into the charcoal from the top. It would be allowed to run until the water was no longer a muddy brown color but crystal clear. The process usually took anywhere from fifteen minutes to half an hour depending on how dirty the filters were. Meanwhile, the aluminum sulfate should be running and the flow of soda ash should be increased to a rate of 4 bags of soda ash to one bag of aluminum sulfate. When the back wash is completed, the aluminum sulfate continues until 4 or 5 hundred pounds has run, then it's turned off and the soda ash releases 100 pounds over an 8 hour period. Once every hour, we take a reading or test the water to keep up with the chlorine and soda ash content in the water. The filter plant is normally operated 24 hours a day.

When we first filled the pool, the water came out of the supply valve a muddy brown, but by Friday, it was crystal clear. Although opening day was still a full week away the pool was full of swimmers who climbed the fence to steal a swim. The two life guards who had been assigned to keep people out had their work cut out for them most of the time. While they chased the people out at one end of the pool, others climbed in from the other end. So they ran back and forth from end to end all day. Besides Frank and me, we had one other guy, Pete Suchanick, who started two days before opening day. He was a student at City College and was planning to be a weather man on TV when he finished school. Starting on opening day, Frank would work from 8 a.m. to 4 p.m. at which time I would relieve him. I would in turn be relieved at 12 midnight by Pete.

The pool was only opened for weekends up until the time school was closed for the summer. Although we worked around the clock seven days a week, we didn't have too much to do and the job was rather boring from time to time. We would take turns back washing which only takes about 2 hours. Otherwise, we just threw in a bag of chemicals and kept an eye on the readings. The foreman came over to sign the report sheets twice a day and to ask questions pertaining to the operation of the filter plant. It seems that he was supposed to be studying for some kind of promotional exam and it was necessary for him to know all aspects of the operations of the pool. He was a rather nervous little fellow. Whenever some high official from the Arsenal came over to inspect the facility, he really got to clicking his heels and saluting and going on. One day about 11 a.m., someone noticed a body at the bottom of the deep pool. It was a seventeen year old boy who wasn't allowed to use the pool because he was an epileptic. However he must have climbed over sometime during the night and probably had a seizure after he jumped into the pool.

I have to say that working at the pool was more of a vacation or should I say it was the closest thing to a vacation with pay that I ever got during my eight years. After killing myself all winter at the rink for 6 days a week and for six months, I think they could have given me something more to do. Not too many things happened of interest at the pool and to me, the ice rink was a far more exciting and challenging job. On 95 degree hot days, the pool was packed to capacity and Sunset was known to have the second highest attendance of all city pools with Astoria having the highest. Cops came around to beg for chemicals as well as advice on how to use them in their backyard pools. One cop took home a jar of calcium hypochlorite (HTH) and stored it in his wife's laundry room next to a bottle of ammonia which his wife had left the cap off. The fumes from the ammonia made contact with the HTH which is contained in a plastic jar. Well the jar melted down and the resulting gas created from the mixture of those two chemicals killed his dog which was locked in the wash room and when the white smoke or gas reached the upper floors where most of his family was asleep, he thought the house was on fire and called the fire dept. This was the correct thing to do, as they're the only ones with the proper gas masks capable of handling this type of situation.

Would you believe he came back the very next day and asked for another jar of the HTH. Speaking of gas masks, the ones we use in the filter house aren't even adequate for handling chlorine. That is to say, it's only good up to 68 parts of gas in the air and the fire dept. says we really shouldn't use them. It's no use trying to tell the higher-ups to buy ones that are recommended by the company that makes the chlorinators. They don't spend much money on essential equipment. Frank told me not to leave anything in sight whenever the plumbers came around from the Five Borough shop because there was one guy who would take everything that was not nailed down including whole cases of HTH, towels or even empty soda ash bags. There was also an electrician from the shops who was always stoned out of his mind or suffering from a hangover from the night before. His partner was doing all the work while he was asleep in the back of the truck. During the course of the summer, groups of school kids from some of the neighborhood summer youth programs came to work at the pool. They were given jobs in many pools as well as other park facilities. At our pool, they were supposed to be painting the fence but each guy just stood in one place most of the day, lifting his paint brush against the fence and then let his arm fall limply down and maybe a little paint came in contact with the fence. There was one guy named Bernard who would bring all the people he could over the fence during a crowded session when he thought the foreman wasn't noticing. He would charge them for coming in. As soon as they went out to swim, he would take whatever valuables or money they had in their pockets and disappear.

During the summer, I decided to try to continue my so far, vain effort to get into show business. After all, that was the reason I came to New York in the first place. I first started writing songs and singing when I was back, home on the farm. Someone told me, "You have to go to New York if you want to be a singer!"

So I came to New York and started singing in amateur shows around the city. After paying admission, I usually ended up sitting around until 1 or 2 in the morning until everyone was half drunk and didn't care what they heard, at which point the M.C. would invite me up on the band stand. Once a week, the MC and one of his associates would rent a studio and hold what they called voice training sessions. The studio consisted of a small dilapidated room in which there was a broken down piano. The building which was on Broadway down around 50th Street should have also been condemned. Anyway, the MC and his associate would charge all 25 of us over-enthusiastic-up-and-coming-young-super-stars-of-the-future, $5 a piece which we readily plunked down, believing that our voice training and good faithful and trusting friend, the MC would one day lead us into spotlights and elevate us to the zenith of fame and stardom. Well, fat chance! I wound up becoming a skate guard. I once answered an ad in the newspaper for young talent. After going to a hotel auditorium, a guy charged me and everyone else $10 just to audition, after which he invited me to come to a church the next day. "Well" I thought, "first he robs me in a hotel and now he wants to rob me in a church."

My cousin Steve, also a country boy, had showbiz in his blood. I thought I would be glad when he got it out of his system so he could stop giving away his money. I decided to make one last desperate effort. I was saving all my money from the pool to pay for a recording session. I was scheduled to start rehearsing around the second week in July. I had two friends who were music arrangers, so I spoke to them about arranging to rehearse some of my originals songs with them and three chorus girls they knew. I finally had everything arranged to start rehearsals for recording at the recording studio.

Connie wanted me to take her to the World's Fair. I had to ask Frank if he would work my shift for me and I would do the same for him whenever he wanted to be off. It was the only possible way to get a day off. No one is allowed to call in sick as that only throws the load on the next guy. After walking all over the World's Fair with Connie and getting blisters all over her feet, I started the first rehearsal session with Wade and Woody, the two music arrangers. Wade played the piano and Woody played the guitar. We rehearsed three songs that I had written and one that Woody wrote. The background singers were friends of Wade and Woody and worked in their band from time to time. We rehearsed for two weeks, 5 days a week for around three hours a day until Wade was satisfied. I then booked the studio on a Friday for a session to be held on the following Wednesday. The song, I wrote was "Burning Tear Drops," was a slow song. We made about six takes of the song and then did one for the B-side, "Like a Movie Star'." This was sung as a fast catchy number and was supposed to really knock them dead. After that, we did one of Woody's tunes, a slow ballad called "Grieving for you." For the

B-side, we used a song that I had written about my brother and his girl and it was called "Poor Dave."

This one didn't quite turn out the way I wanted it to. In fact, none of them quite turned out the way I expected. We were in the studio for three hours, running tapes at $45 an hour. In addition, I had a five piece band in which each man received $35 an hour. The three chorus girls each received $25 an hour, plus another $60 for the tape and $35 for the records. Altogether, I spent around $900 or more by the end of the day. I spent much of the summer peddling my records around to every record company in the city. Many of them kept my records for three weeks and returned them via the mail with a note stating, "Thanks for your interest in our company but . . . etc." Or, I would step off the elevator at the offices of a big record company and the receptionist would greet me with a broad smile on her face. When I asked to see the A & R Director she would say, "Oh he's in conference today" or "He's out of town for two weeks." I was getting no place fast, so I decided that maybe if I left them at some big companies that had a number of top line artists, they might be interested in having their people record them and I could make money from the royalties as a song writer.

Woody and I took care of the copyright and then I went to Atlantic Records. They wouldn't even let me in the door. I had a copy of the mono-tape I made and sent it to Berry Gordy of Motown Records in Detroit. I never received a reply, nor did they even return the tape. I never especially liked the way night clubs smelled, nor did I really care for the type of people that one generally found in night clubs. I decided to give up my singing career. Anyway, it wasn't too bad being a skate guard.

My Swiss Miss

So charming, so sweet, so innocent
Sensitive fingers of your being
Touched my feelings and made them soft
I want to laugh and sing and cry
You hold the key to my very being
You came so suddenly to shine your light
Divine and soothing into forgotten corners of my heart
Too suddenly my love, your love potion found its mark
Susanne . . . . I love you

CHAPTER IV

The swimming season dragged on and was about to come to a close when one day in late August, I received a call from my cousin who informed me that my grandfather, who had raised me since I was 2 years old, had passed away of a heart attack. It was a big shock. My grandfather taught me how to work and not to be afraid of work, to earn everything I get, to always try to have something of my own, not to envy things that belong to others, and most important, show the utmost respect and consideration for old people. In addition, he said, stay away from "bad company," it'll keep you out of trouble. I live by these basic principles today. It was inconceivable that he was gone. It was like waking up one day and finding that the mountain that had stood for ages was suddenly just not there anymore. Mr. George Brown, December 9, 1886 – August 26, 1965. Although I hadn't been home in more than 6 years, we wrote to each other often. I will always have the highest regard and the deepest love for him. My cousin also told me that he had been asking about me just before he died and wanted to see me. Well, the only thing I could do was resign and leave for Georgia. The funeral was scheduled for Sunday and there was only one week left in the season. I bought an airline ticket and flew down to Tallahassee after changing in Atlanta.

My relatives picked me up from the Tallahassee, Fla. Airport and then drove to Cairo GA. I met all my ninety-nine hundred relatives whom I hadn't seen in 5 or 6 years. Many of them came from Florida, Michigan, Pennsylvania and West Virginia. The funeral service was so sad and well attended by many friends and neighbors from the surrounding areas and my family. The church was completely filled. My grandmother received a tranquilizer from her doctor and managed well doing the service. I felt completely empty inside. The saddest part of the service was at the grave site when the preacher said, "Ashes to ashes and dust to dust," and lowered the casket into the vault. After the funeral everyone returned to the house which was about 2 miles from the church. All my aunts were in the kitchen cooking and preparing food for all the people that attended the service. Many of the neighbors brought cakes, pies, fried chicken and covered casserole dishes as they came to pay their respects.

Later during the week, I was walking around and looking over the old place and reliving all of my childhood memories, becoming enveloped in all the old sights, sounds and smells. They sent me flashing back to an almost forgotten childhood. The old man didn't do much farming since my brothers and I left home. He only had about 2 acres of corn planted in the Sugar Mill Yard. All the rest of the land, about 125 acres, had been rented out to other farmers for the past few years. When I was younger, he used to tell me that "One day this place will belong to you." At the time, I was too young to understand and ran away from home the first chance I got. I was supposed to bring in that last field of corn for grandma, but by the time I had gathered half of it, I came down with the worst asthma attack I had had since the days when I was young and living on the farm. The dust from the plants and grain will usually bring on a violent attack and I would have to sleep nights sitting up in a chair, working hard to draw in each breath and forcing it out again. This could continue for as long as 2 weeks and as far as I knew, no doctor has been able to do anything about it. It was especially bad during the months of September to April.

So, I figured the best thing I could do was to take a Greyhound bus and head back to New York. 28 hours after I said goodbye to the folks in Cairo and climbed aboard, I was pulling into the Port Authority Bus Terminal in New York. There was only a small reminder of my asthma attack. I guess New York City's air pollution is a little more suitable to my respiratory system. When I got home to Brooklyn, Mama Sara, my landlord, informed me that someone had called me from Wollman Rink the day before and that I was to report there on the following Monday. Bright and early Monday morning, I was happily on my way to the rink. Mr. Joe Dee was there well dressed, unperturbed and looking very official as usual. In his soft spoken manner, he shook my hand and said, "Marvin, I'm glad to see you, how are you doing? Did you have a good summer?" I assured him that I was fine and that my summer was quite good. Of course, I was quite surprised that he would greet me with what I thought was such warm interest. Not many of last season's crew was there. Al Erber was in the army and George Finlayson got married and moved to New Jersey to sell vacuum cleaners and washing machines for Sears Roebuck. Walter Shumway opened his own Judo School in New City, NY. Many others had gone on to bigger and better things. However, Greg and I were still there and so were Chino, Billy Davis and Bobby Parker from last year's night crew. This year we're going to have Uncle Rudy as our chief. He worked on the night crew for many seasons as a skate guard. During the summer, he rode bicycles in a club where he trained other riders. We were all sent up to the Arsenal for appointments.

After filling out the necessary forms, we gave them to Mr. Callender who was the finger-print man. He refused to accept them because they weren't completed properly. Some of us had to go back 2 or 3 times because we missed something or forgot to put down the date. After we were fingerprinted, we had to wait until Mrs. Williams called us up to the window to pay the 15 cents fingerprint fee. Next we waited on the bench outside Mr. Veackie's office, waiting to see him to finish the paperwork. When called in, we would sit while he rambled through his eternal pile of papers on his desk. I asked somebody why he didn't retire. The reply was that he had retired 3 or 4 times, but he always managed to wrangle his way back into the job because he had many friends with influence at City Hall. "Next," yelled Mr. Veackie finally. After we had all been through Mr. Veackie's office, we returned to the rink and Mr. Joe Dee said, "All of you new guys report on Friday at 12 o'clock, at which time you'll be given uniforms and told when to report to work. All of you guys from the previous season will start work immediately."

We pulled out the hose and got busy washing down the slab which is the first step in preparation for making ice. After the supervisor was satisfied that the slab was clean enough, he had us bring up a 55-gallon drum from the refrigeration plant which we used to mix up the white wash. White wash is used to paint the slab white so that the slab reflects the sunrays instead of absorbing them and melting the ice. Mr. Joe Dee supervised every detail. Some of us dashed buckets of white wash onto the slab while others used push brooms to spread this liquid mess evenly over the entire slab. The engineer had already put his refrigeration plant into operation and the white wash was starting to take up or freeze solid.

After the white wash had frozen solid all over, we pulled the hose out and started to spray water on the washed slab, and thus were putting down the first layer of ice on top of which we continued to build it up until we had half an inch in places and one inch in others. We had to work overtime. The best time to build ice is after sundown and at night. After the first couple of sprays over the slab, we removed our hip boots and put on our skates. We worked until around 11 p.m. and were given the next day off. Although, we didn't quite complete 16 hours of work, we don't get paid for overtime, we have what they call time coming. For every 8 hours of overtime, we get a day off even though we would prefer the money. Some of the guys have built up as much as 2 weeks of overtime leave by the end of the season. They just take the last 2 weeks off. We're also supposed to get supper money, around $3 every time we work more than 2 hours overtime. However, Mr. Joe Dee put an end to that. After taking our day off, we came in on the following morning which was Wednesday and got busy laying rubber mats around the boardwalk. That took all day. Then on Thursday, we washed all the windows. On Friday morning, we went up for uniforms before the crowd of new guys, who were to come in at noon and get their uniforms. Saturday morning was opening day and the season was off to a merry start.

At conditioning time, Uncle Rudy wanted us to pan, spray and squeegee. Mr. Joe Dee wanted the ice cut and he ordered Uncle

Rudy to do that. We pulled out the equipment and Uncle Rudy seemed angry because we had to cut the ice. He would snap at us every now and then and yell, "Come on, let's go, you're not on vacation you bunch of lackeys!" This couldn't apply to me because I was driving the tractor and plowing the snow into the pit. Greg was working the plow with his pan. When we finished he looked quite tired as he said, "I don't understand why the hell, they don't get us a Zamboni to do the work for us. You know what I mean Ace?" I agreed that we should have a Zamboni like the rink in Brooklyn. A Zamboni is a machine that cuts the ice, picks up the snow shavings and puts down a layer of water all at the same time. However, our rink wasn't level and I heard it said a number of times that in order to use a Zamboni machine, the rink must be level.

Billy Davis landed a job with the Monuments Division. A job he had applied for a couple of years ago. His new job entailed scraping the pigeon droppings from the statues that are located all over town. He was quite happy in his new work as the pay was twice that of a skate guard. Bobby Parker landed a job as a plumber at New York University Hospital. Chino captured the heart of one of those rich middle aged ladies from the morning session. He can be seen stepping in and out of a chauffeured Rolls Royce along 5th Avenue from time to time. Yes, it looked as though everybody was moving up except me. Uncle Rudy was almost constantly in conflict with Mr. Joe Dee, so he decided the best thing for him to do was to resign. After all he wasn't working because he needed the money. He had plenty of stocks and bonds, real estate, etc. He said, he worked during the winter because it was too cold to ride his bicycle the winter months. He felt that if the supervisor is going to come out every time and tell him what to do, then the supervisor didn't really need a chief, who is supposed to be responsible for the ice and the guards patrolling the ice.

Uncle Rudy put in his resignation for the coming Friday which was the end of the pay week. Meanwhile, he just played the game until Friday and did whatever the boss said should be done. Greg and I spent a lot of time trying to figure out who would be the next chief. Just about all the guys with many years of experience had already moved on to greater heights. The only guy left from the old days was Bob Tom on the night crew. We decided that Bob Tom was the man. However, on Saturday morning when we came in, the ice was all ready as the night crew had cut the night before and one guy had stayed overnight and sprayed to build ice. So we all went up for breakfast and came back. Bob Tom wasn't there. We were sitting around in the locker room and Mr. Joe Dee came in and said, "Good morning fellas," and I just couldn't get ready for what he said next. "Fellas, starting right now, Marvin Brown is your chief. You'll take orders and respect him as such. Any man disrespecting him or is noticed doing his job grudgingly will have to see me. All the chief has to do is let me know and I'll have a piece of paper for that man to sign, namely, a resignation slip. Now Marvin the first thing you have to do is put a man out there to watch those figure club kids. There's a man sleeping over there in the corner. Wake him up." In his soft spoken voice he continued, "Now Marvin, if you have any problems you just come in to see me and let me know and we'll try to solve them together."

With this he left the locker room. I was in shock but I came out of it just long enough to wake up the guy sleeping in the corner. He was one of the new guys named Bobby McDougal. I woke him up and informed him that I was his boss from now on and that he was going to have to shape up or ship out. He finally finished putting on his uniform and skates after moving around like he was held together with scotch tape. Afterwards, I just sort of walked around in a stupor for the next couple of hours trying to figure out what to do next. I felt like someone had hit me over the head with something and my head had gotten very big. Instead of a $12 a day skate guard, I was now a $13 a day chief. Well, if I must be the boss, then I'll be the boss. Actually, there was nothing to do as the Von's kids had the ice until the free session started. There was a crowd gathering outside and well, I guess the only thing to do is open the gate and let them in. I asked Greg to watch the gate, where I also spent a lot of time. I asked him why the boss didn't make him the chief instead of me.

"Well, I don't know Ace, but I wouldn't have taken it anyway. That job, Ace, is too much of a headache. Anyway, I find it easier to do as I'm told." After eight years of working as a skate guard, I can agree with him. Needless to say, Bob Tom and a few others felt they had been cheated and were quite resentful of my appointment as chief instead of them. They felt that they had more years on the job and were far better qualified to be the chief than I was. I would have been the first to agree with them. Mr. Joe Dee called me into the office during lunch time and said, "Marvin I picked you for the job because you're a good man, a hard worker. You're dependable and never absent or late, plus you're serious and you take interest in your job and I like that.

I think those are very good qualities and indicate a responsible person." I nodded in modest agreement and he continued, "I have a lot of confidence in you and I'm sure you're going to make a good chief. By the way how is your leg?"

"Oh, it's as good as new." That was probably the biggest lie I ever told. My knee protests whenever I overwork it. He finished by saying that he thought it would be a good idea to cut the ice after the speed session. At the end of the speed session, I got on the PA system to make the necessary announcement. We all went out to do the ice. I had already changed the blade in the cutter and I had Greg driving the jeep with one of the new guys boxing. His name was Gill. I had trouble adjusting the cutter as I had never operated the cutter before and no one ever offered to teach me. It's supposed to be adjusted to cut from the right side of the machine close against the rail the first time around, after which it's readjusted to cut from left side, leaving a small ridge where the end of the cutting blade passes through the ice. This ridge is then cut away by the bow in the center of the blade.

The machine can be adjusted so that after the blade is mounted on, the blade is dipped at the center mounting bolt. The bow is visible and if too much bow is put in, you can wind up cutting too much ice from the center of the blade and not enough or none at all from the outside. I didn't know all of that, so I just cut and the ridge that was supposed to be cut out each time around was so far, eluding the blade altogether. After I finished the ice and Greg pushed away the rest of the snow with the jeep, he backed it into the garage and came into the locker room and said, "Ace boy I swear, your ice looks like a wood screw turned upside down."

The rest of the crew and me fell over laughing. Greg continued, "You know there was a guy out all night long building up the ice you ripped off. Man you cut so deep, the engineer came running upstairs with a crew cut." I sent everybody onto the ice to keep the people off until it was 2:30. In addition, there were barriers to be placed across the pit. I skated around to see if there were any very low spots. What I found were places where the blade had cut under the ice and bit into the concrete. I had someone get a bucket of water to pour on it and Greg was saying something about watching out and not to fall over my own ridges, or did he say cliffs. During the session, I didn't have to skate if I didn't want to, as long as I made sure that everyone else was on the ice. But since it was a weekend session, I figured, I should put my skates on and remain in a strategic area so that I could be ready to lend myself to any situation that might develop. Mr. Joe Dee came out to where I was standing in front of the garage and asked, "Marvin how are you doing? Is everything alright?" Before I could figure out if everything was alright, he turned to face the ice and said, "That was a very nice cut you made . . . of course there are a few ridges here and there but they'll skate them off in no time." I told him that there were no problems so far, to which he replied, "Good, that's very good." He went back into the office and resumed his phone conversation.

Connie was meeting me after work and we were supposed to go to see a movie. Before she got there however, I was almost tempted to going home with a rather fine looking German airline stewardess named Reanata, who had been trying to lure me away from the ice each time she came down. This time I almost gave in. If only Connie had been a little bit late, I would probably have wound up some place learning German and other things. Connie came and we went to the movies and afterwards to a Chinese restaurant to celebrate my new status. It snowed that night and the next morning. I really had my work cut out for me. We canceled the figure skating and dance session and we used the jeep to push all the snow to the back part of the rink. We worked to get 2/3 of the ice clean and ready to open the rink. By 10 a.m. the line was already forming. Many people were heard complaining that those lazy skate guards should have gotten out of bed early enough to have the ice ready for the figure and dance session because it was Sunday morning and they had looked forward to going skating.

Oh well, some people go to church and others worship the ice. We took a cut and with a tremendous effort managed to get ¾ of the ice ready by 10 a.m. I have always thought that the city should have built a dome over the rink. But then, they probably didn't want to spend the money as usual. After the session commenced, I continued to push the snow from the back of the rink into the pit, with one guy helping me and the others skating the session. My ice cutting skills developed more and more with each cut I made. I talked to Frenchie every chance I got, to pick up a few tips. I soon had the whole thing down to a science. Mr. Joe Dee would come to me every now and then just before conditioning time and ask, "Marvin what do you think you ought to do to the ice?" I would tell him what I had planned for reconditioning and he would reply, "That's fine, very good. That's exactly what I was thinking."

For some reason, he never bothered me the way he did Uncle Rudy and we actually got along quite well. He would tell me that

I didn't have to go out and help my crew pan the rink or help them to clean the pit. After all, I was their boss. But I always felt that even though I was their boss, I would never send any of them out to do anything that I wouldn't do myself. Of course, I was glad to go out and work alongside the crew as I figured they would finish what they were doing that much quicker and they would all have that much more time to relax after they finished. Besides, I figured it was the only way for me to always know exactly what was going on. When comparing this particular crew with the ones I had in later sessions, I have to in all fairness say that my first crew was the best of them all. But then the crew is only as good as its chief, who in turn is only as good as the supervisor. So perhaps, I too went downhill in later years. Every Sunday morning, we would have uniform inspection to make sure that everyone had gotten his uniform cleaned and pressed and polished his skates. The crew would all line up side by side on the ice to exhibit their uniforms. Gill with his broad shoulders and mischievous smile had a big gap between his two front teeth. Bobby, who stood tall, always kept his eyes squinted and looked sleepy most of the time. His hair was so thick that his hat could barely sit on top of his head. Rex always looked very professional. Joe Rivera had a rather calm philosophical face. Greg was always happy and tried to make everybody that way by keeping them laughing. Eddie Parrot, who seemed to be in full flight around the rink when he was skating, was definitely in full flight in the park on his racing bicycle. Tommy Lin was very honorable. James McCoy was fascinated with the army and good things to eat. Peanut, although he was only a couple of feet tall and looked like a six year old, was actually a couple of years older than me. Lastly, Beno Thomas skated like a chicken and had a beard that made him look like Abe Lincoln. There they all stood, Wollman's finest and I have to admit that I felt quite proud of them myself, "The prefect crew."

While I was engaged in clearing away the snow, I had a line of yellow rubber cones placed across the rink to indicate to the skaters that this was as far back as they're allowed to skate, and also to keep them out of the path of the jeep while I was working. However, there is always at least one person who will insist on breaking the rules. This time it was a cute little French girl, named Simone. After chasing her away a number of times, I asked her, how would you feel if I accidently ran over you? "I don't seeink you weel hurt me!" I told her that it was a good thing the session ended in five minutes. I would at last be rid of her. To which she replied, "Oh I weel come in zee afternoon also." "Don't you do anything else besides going skating?"

Yes but eet ez my day off and I don't have eenezeng to do!" "I see." I bid her good day and went into the office to call an end to the session. The crew and I went out and did the ice. Most of the crew said it was a perfect cut with the exception of a couple of ridges. This time, we opened up the entire rink. The music started and the crowd descended on to the ice like a swarm of hungry locusts. The French girl was among them. She came to pester me again. "Hello monsieur I am here again!" "So I see." I responded, "Do you represent

Paris? "No, Brest!" I must say, Brest was well represented. "Will you skate weez me?" "Well no, I'm not allowed to skate with anyone." "Why eez zat?" "The boss might think I'm having a good time." "Do you not have . . . . what you say . . . good time?" "Yes, only at times like now when things start getting interesting!" Eenterezting, what eez zat?" "That's how my job is sometimes." I was skating around and she skated next to me. I asked her what she did for a living. "I zeet weez a baby for a family." She was short and had such a happy smile and fascinating eyes that seemed to dance whenever she smiled and yes, a Napoleon styled haircut, short and close to her head. After I finished work, I invited her to see a movie.

The season dragged on and so did the girls, which I later regarded as the only fringe benefit the job had to offer, or was it an addiction. One Sunday morning Papa Joe, who was the number one man or assistant foreman and unofficial chief of chiefs, decided after a close inspection of the ice that the ice wasn't good enough for the figure and dance session. The night crew cut the ice the night before and left too many corners untouched. The day crew was obligated to correct the problem. We changed the blade and did that. After we finished, Greg came over and said, "Ace you're without a doubt the greatest cut man in the history of Wollman Rink". Knowing Greg the way I do, I figured he was pulling my leg and reminded him that not too long ago he was telling me how terrible my ice was. To which he replied, "Yes, I know I said all that, but now I'm forced to change my opinion. Yah know what I think Ace. I'll bet that one day they're going to call you over to the Arsenal and award you the order of the "Silver Cut Blade." "Yeah Brown," said Parrot, "They are going to decorate you in park leaves." "No wait," said Gill, "They're going to carve a statue of Brown out of ice and erect it over the pit."

"Yeah Brown," said Joe Rivera, "the inscription is going to read, to cut or not to cut. Here stands the sharpest of all blades." "Aw you guys quit the bull and let's go up for breakfast!" Even though I knew they were just putting me on, I was glad that their morale was so high. Then too, the figure skaters seemed happy enough except for a couple who spent most of the session squabbling over a patch of ice that one of them thought they had exclusive rights to.

New Year's Day was the beginning of a subway strike. In order to cope with the problem of getting to work and back, most of the guys decided to sleep over. Greg had his Honda and a couple of other guys had cars. But other than that, everybody rode the subway and buses. The locker room was rather crowded most of the time with the biggest part of both crews having to sleep over. What an odor! I don't think any skate guards had a bath the entire two weeks that the train strike lasted. They slept on top of the lockers, all over the floor and up in the ceiling. Anywhere there was a place to sleep, there was a skate guard sleeping there. They or should I say we spent most of the time sitting around telling jokes. One guy who worked as a life guard during the summer on the Coney Island Beach, told horror stories about a body that had washed ashore one day while he was on duty. It was all bloated up from being in the water for many weeks, and every time a wave came in and pushed against it, the body would shake and bounce like jelly.

Another guy told of a relationship he was having with a girl at his pool and on his day off, he and his wife packed the picnic basket and took their baby and went to the beach. When the girl friend came to the beach and insisted on joining the party, the wife got angry and threw all the food into the ocean and grabbed the baby and ran home. Another told of how he managed to come from Puerto Rico to New York and left running as soon as he got some shoes on his feet. Still somebody else declared that his buddy should go out to the pit and take a bath. "Boy!" said Greg, "I wonder how Frenchie managed to accumulate such a large number of mental midgets for his night crew." After sleeping at the rink for a full week, it was Friday and pay day. I was thinking about trying to get away home so that I might freshen up a bit. Butch and I walked out to the Bank to cash our checks. As we were on our way back up 64th Street, just after we crossed 5th Ave. in the front of the Arsenal, a tall well-dressed man dashed up and grabbed my right hand and started pumping my arm like someone desperately trying to get water out of a dry well. My first thought was, this guy must be trying to get elected to some office and wants me to vote for him. "Hello how are you guys doing? I'm glad to see you and I heard what a great job you're doing down at Wollman. I'm Mr. Thomas Hoving, the new Commissioner of Parks." "Please to meet you," I said, "Yes, we have been sleeping at the rink since the strike started." "Well that's great. I'm very pleased with you fellows and I'm going to send down some more cots so that all of you'll have a place to sleep. Don't you worry fellows. The new Mayor of the City of New York will have this strike settled in no time."

Just as suddenly as he came, he dashed away up the steps of the Arsenal and into the building and disappeared. However, he wasn't called Hoving for nothing. He had been seen a number of times standing up on the deck at 4:00 a.m. in the morning watching whoever was building ice over night. After he had bid us good day, Butch said, "That guy sure act as if he needed some friends." "Yes," I said. He seemed to like skate guards. The Mayor and the unions took care of business and the strike came to an end but not before the all powerful union leader who was responsible for the strike died suddenly of a mysterious heart attack. On a Tuesday, Greg came in and announced that he had been drafted. He was leaving in two weeks and wanted to know if I would buy his bike. "Well what do you say Ace? I'll let you have it for three hundred dollars. I mean after all, I paid six for it." I didn't quite know what to say, as I didn't have three hundred dollars. "Well let me put it this way. If I can get the money from my girl, I'll buy it."

"Ok Ace, but you'll have to let me know by the weekend, so I'll have a chance to sell it to someone else, in case you can't take it." Well, I knew Connie had some money in the bank but I didn't know how much. So, I called her at home and explained the situation and surprisingly she said, "Ok Marv, I'll be right down with the money. You know I'll do just anything for you Marv!" And before the end of the day, Greg and I were up at the 72nd Street parking lot and he was giving me the rundown on the gear shifting techniques which consisted of hand and foot gear levers. Now let's see, was it up for first and down for second, or down for third and up for fourth.

At some point while riding the bike, I decided that where I was going, I must be late because everybody else was coming back. Oh no! Wait. Holy Moses! I'm going the wrong way down a one-way street. That's why everybody was blowing their horns and flashing their lights and waving at me. After regaining my sense of direction for a moment, I promptly lost it again and found myself putting around in lower Chinatown, looking for the approach to Manhattan Bridge to Brooklyn.

I finally arrived home with the motorcycle and parked it in the front of the house inside the gate. Mama Sara happened to come out of the house to empty the garbage at that moment and said, "Boy, what in the world is that you got? That's a motorcycle, aint it?" I assured her that it was. She laughed and fiddled with the handlebars and replied, "These things are dangerous to ride, aint they?" She apparently decided that they were dangerous and went back into the safety of the house, leaving the door open for me. I made sure the gas petcock was off and went inside, prepared my dinner, ate, took a hot bath and got a good night's sleep.

One thing about working at the rink, when you get home, you're usually so tired that when you crawl into bed, you fall into a deep sleep almost immediately, especially after a hot bath. During the summer when I'm not working, I was up and still bubbling over with excitement over my new purchase. Dressed and ready to go, I walked out the front door to be greeted by a merciless Jack Frost who really was taking care of business this day. It was very cold. I put the key into my shiny black and silver Honda 160 and pressed the start button and all it would do was turn over without starting. After about five minutes of that, I figured I should see if I could get Greg on the phone. I did and he said, "Ace I was just about to walk out the door as the phone rang." I told him about the problem I was having starting the motorcycle and he said, "First of all, you must turn on the gas, and secondly you have to flip up the choke lever. Have you done all that?" I shamefacedly admitted that I hadn't, to which he said, "Hell Ace, you'd be turning the motor all day and it never will start."

So I went outside and did all the things Greg said and sure enough it started right up. I hopped on and did battle with Jack Frost all the way to Central Park. When I arrived at the rink and parked the bike under the tree next to the pit, I could hardly walk. I had trouble straightening my knees which had just about frozen solid along with my fingers and toes and jawbone. Once inside the locker room, I sat on top of the radiator for an half an hour to thaw myself out.

Greg came in shortly and said, "Ace man let me tell you, it's colder than a witch's toes. I mean to say that old Jack Frost is really kicking ass out there today." We sprayed and squeegeed the ice and went up for breakfast. During the session, I decided that since it was so cold, I should send out only two guys for fifteen minutes at the time and relieve them by two others. Friday was Greg's last day on the job and we all chipped in and brought a bottle of good cognac to toast Greg and wish him luck and a safe return. He only made a joke of the whole affair. His girl friend, Joan was also there and her eyes looked as though she'd been crying. She was hanging around his waist. "Well fellas, Joan might have me today, but Uncle Sam is going to have me tomorrow." After he said this Joan burst into tears. "They're going to send me over to Vietnam, to get shot at, cut at, hit at and missed. I hope I'm missed." "Oh boo hoo, bawled Joan, "Stop it please, Greg. You don't know how you make me feel." The party ended and although Greg came down a couple of times the following week, I didn't see him again until the beginning of the summer. That season drew to a close and Mr. Joe Dee bid us farewell until next October. We were all reassigned after being told we must take a week off so that we had a break in service, otherwise if we managed to work a complete year with no break in service, they would have to give us a vacation with pay, and that just couldn't be tolerated. Whoever heard of a seasonal worker getting vacation pay.

In the middle of the season, one skate guard, Pete Colon died of aids. He had been with us for many years working first at Wollman and later at Lasker Ice Rink. He was a good worker, loved and dependable. He was also a drug user as well as a number of the other guys. This is probably how he contracted the HIV virus. I believe the virus was created by two scientists in a lab here in this country in the 1960's. It was created to be used to wipe out the people of Vietnam. But first, it had to be tested to make sure it worked. So they took it to Africa and injected an entire village with it which started the epidemic that decimated the population of Africa. The only monkeys involved were the two who worked in the Lab. All the other monkeys are innocent.

Marvin Brown and the coworker Angel Cruz

TRIBUTE TO A CHIEF

The job you do is trying,
To all your inner skill,
It won't get done by crying,
You need an iron will.
The work is quite demanding,
At any given time,
The crew needs understanding.
Be everything they need,
Their doctor, lawyer, priest,
Their mother, father, police,
They always look to you,
You are their supreme chief.

I was assigned to the 97th Street baseball fields along with one of my crew members, Bobby McDougal. Our job required us to report to work at 4 p.m. The job consisted of turning on the spot lights for the Goya League teams that played baseball at night. We cleaned up, in and around the building and then we went down to turn off the lights after the teams had finished. We would then go back to the baseball house and wait for each team to turn in their bases. However, the teams themselves spent more time batting each other over the head than they did batting the ball. The pitcher would throw a badly thrown ball toward home plate and hit the guy at bat. He would get angry and go storming out after the pitcher. While they were wrapped tightly around each other, the members of both teams would grab a bat and proceed to hit each other over the heads.

And all their relatives as well would come charging down from the bleachers to get in a few hard knocks. There would be such rolling, tumbling and kicking up great clouds of dust. One evening, Bob and I were standing a little beyond the fence along the ball field when I noticed that one out of every three balls knocked out of bounds would fall within a few feet of where we were standing and they had plenty of speed behind them. So, I said to Bob, maybe we should move back a little past the edge of the fence to which he replied, "Man them lemons better not hit me!" However, I would rather be safe than sorry so, I moved back and sure enough the very next foul ball caught Bob right in the mouth. His lip was cut and he had to go to Roosevelt Hospital for stitches. One day, I had to take off from work to go to the Compensation Board about my knee accident.

When I arrived down town Manhattan at 50 Park Place, I spent most of the day just sitting around. When my turn finally came, I was asked a few questions by a judge or referee as he was called, and whenever I gave an answer, there were two shabbily dressed men sitting to my left, objecting to everything I said. So, I inquired as to why they were objecting, as I was only relating exactly what happened. The referee instructed me to pay no attention to them and that their objections didn't mean anything because they're only there to defend the city. I was sent to a different part of the building to be examined by doctors. Then, I returned to part 12, as it was called, where I just sat around and waited some more. I was finally called in again, this time by the referee. He said my name and began reading from a piece of paper. What he read sounded to me like he was reading from the Bible using such words as "hereof" and "henceforth" and "whereas" or something like that. Anyway, I didn't know what the heck he was talking about until he read a part that said "$28 per week for . . .", I didn't remember how many weeks, but he said something about 15% loss of use in the left knee. So, to get a little better understanding I asked, "How much is that going to be?" To which he replied, "We don't do arithmetic. You'll receive a check in the mail in about 2 weeks." And sure enough, 10 days later I got a brown envelope in the mail and it contained a check for $1300. Well, I decided right then that my current bike and grown too small and no longer measured up to my abilities as a bike enthusiast. Anyway, I had a chance once or twice, to ride behind a guy named Fearless Dave O'Sullivan. He rode a 250 Ducati and my little Honda just couldn't keep him in sight whenever we rode around the park. So, I cashed my check and I went to Camrod & Rods, a West Side Ducati Dealer.

After choosing the Ducati I wanted, I plunked down $700 for the new bike which cost $900. I was allowed $200 for my old bike. It was 9 am when I arrived and paid for the new bike and 6 p.m. before they made any effort to get the bike ready. I later learned that the first thing you don't do is pay them for the bike the minute you walk into the place because once they have your money tucked safely into the cash register, they forget you exist. I also learned that they charged me $200 more than what the bike should have cost. What a rude awakening. They saw me coming. I vowed never to do business with them again and have since brought two other bikes from a more reputable dealer. Little did I realize that the only thing those bikes had in store for me was a lot of trouble.

The time came for us all to be reappointed for the pools and this time the Parks Department had a surprise for me. Instead of being sent to Sunset Pool, I was being sent to McCarren Pool which was located way out in Greenpoint. This pool was all the way out in the woods. So, I called the chief engineer at Randalls Island and asked why I was being sent out there. He informed me that they were seriously short of experienced help and I was to go to McCarren as the number one man. I would be in charge of training two new guys that they were sending later in the week and if I didn't like that arrangement, I could quit. I assured him that I was quite happy with the arrangement and set out to find McCarren Park. But not before I had a chance to tackle Fearless Dave around the park on my new Ducati, I was stopped for a light in the park and he pulled up next to me and revved his engine a couple of times. When he realized it was me and on a brand new bike, the same as his, he was going to teach me a thing or two about how to ride a Ducati.

The light changed and we both revved up and dropped the clutch and red lined the tachometer. With his long hair waving in the wind like a wild horse's mane and crouched over like Mike the Bike Hailwood and moving like greased lightening, he was gone. After he went around the first turn, I didn't even know which way he went. On the other hand, my bike was still new and not yet broken in. I exited from the park at 72nd Street and headed over to 2nd Avenue and down to the Williamsburg Bridge. I found my way to the pool and introduced myself to the supervisor. My starting date was the next day. I arrived at the pool at 8 a.m. and asked the foreman for the key to the filter house. He told me that another filter plant operator had reported for work half an hour before I got there and that he took the keys and was already in the filter house. I walked across the pool to the other side and entered the filter house. I had my shoulder bag which I normally carry and had intended to put it in the locker that I had picked out the day before and was the best locker of the three. Well, whoever he was, he was nowhere to be seen and plus he had put a lock on my chosen locker. Half an hour later, the gate opened and a short well-dressed slick looking character walked in and informed me that he was Tony Kastbaloni and that his "fader" was a supervisor in the Five-Borough Shops. Also, he was going to be the number one man and that he was going to work midnight to eight. I stared at him in amazement and said, "You're going to do what?" He explained very forcefully, "I'm going to work midnight to eight, because my fader got me this job and he's one of the big bosses in the shops and what he says, goes and I ain't working no other shift."

"What pool did you work in last year?" I asked. "I never worked in a pool before." Well, how about that. First, they send me way out here in the middle of nowhere and then they add insult to injury. They think they can send some wet-nosed, poker-face kid over here who doesn't know a valve stem from a hole in the ground and the first thing he does is take my locker and then tell me what he ain't going to do. I'm supposed to teach him how to be my boss. Well, we shall see about that. I inquired as to whether or not his FADER was going to teach him how to run the plant, so he could be the number one man. Then he said, "Somebody named Brown is going to teach me how to run it." "Oh, yeah! Well I'm Brown. I have worked at a pool before. I'm number one man and I most definitely am going to work midnight to eight!!!! "Yeah well, my fader said I was to work that shift." "Well your fader is a boss on Randall's Island and you're working over here. And anyway, I don't care what your fader said." "You can't do this to me, my fader worked for the city for 25 years. He got lots of pull and he'll have you out in the park picking papers before opening day." "Like I said, I'm number one man here and our first job is to change the bulbs in those two islands in the pool."

I went over to the office to get the necessary tools. I gave him what he needed to work with except a ladder which I told him to look for himself. We normally work together in the island, but I decided very quickly that this princeling son of the "all conquering Randall's Island boss" will learn that his daddy can't help him today. I mean it's ok to fix a job for your son, your nephew or the kid next door, but don't send him out to the place and tell him that he's going to be the big shot or to disregard the guys that have been there for years. Let him have the job, but let him know he has to follow the rules. By the time he got the top of his island off, I was half finished with mine. Ten minutes after he climbed down inside, he came over to complain that someone had put the nuts on the fixtures too tight and that it was too hot and dirty inside there. I explained that he must climb back down inside there and back those wing nuts off with the pliers, pry, the fixtures out with the screwdriver, screw out the old bulb and screw in the new one and replace everything the way it was.

Well, he climbed back down inside as he mumbled something about his "fader" said there was nothing to do on this job but just sit around. So I told him, if he wanted a job sitting around he would have to go out to Randall's Island and work for his "fader." Well, it was just too goddamn bad about him. If he was going to work with me, he was going to bloody well earn his keep. He thought he had a job where all he had to do was just sign the blotter and collect his check. Well, from that day forward, I intended to make sure he earned every cotton-picking penny of it. And I didn't give a good goddamn, if his pappy was the Mayor or the Governor.

CHAPTER V

His suit was ripped in a couple of places and covered with rust and corrosion and spider webs. I didn't understand why he didn't bring work clothes. But then, he only planned to just sit around. He left saying, "My "fader" is going to hear about this." I knew from the start he couldn't do a days work in a month. I decided that maybe I would feel sorry for him. The next day, I wound up changing the bulbs myself.

After work, I thought I might give my new bike a little more breaking-in mileage. So I took a ride out to Long Island with the intention of ending up at Ghost Motorcycles in Port Washington. Only thing, I got lost and ended up somewhere on the wrong parkway. At one point, a white car pulled up next to me and a voice yelled, "Pull over," through a loud speaker which was mounted to the fender. I did that and the car which turned out to be a police car, stopped in front of me. A cop got out and demanded my license and registration without informing me what I had done wrong. He started back to his car and stopped halfway and growled, "I'm going to give you a speeding ticket." Before I had a chance to protest he got into his car and started writing. Well if THAT didn't beat all. Well, I knew my bike was plenty fast, but I wasn't going any faster than the car ahead of me and he was giving me a speeding ticket. Oh well, it had been a bad day right from the start. After I received my speeding ticket, the cop drove away spinning up clouds of dust from the shoulder of the road. The ticket read that I was doing 60 in a 50 mph zone and that I had to answer it in a place called Mineola, wherever that was.

If I was doing 60, then so was the car ahead of me. Well, in any case, he won't have to worry about me anymore, I will never grace this highway again with my new bike. I stumbled around in the wilderness until I came upon a sign that read, "Belt Parkway, Brooklyn." I stopped at Nathan's in Coney Island and had couple of franks, french fries and a grape soda. Then I went home. Fearless Dave O'Sullivan worked for a motorcycle messenger service and he told me that he could get me a job there, if I was interested. I told him that I was and would be ready to start as soon as I got my pool filled and into operation. Then I would take the midnight shift and this would leave me free during the day to take an extra job.

However, I first had to deal with this "fader" and son situation. When I arrived at work Monday morning and as I came into the office to sign in there was this Tony character drinking coffee with the supervisor and really buttering him up, or as we say at the rink, brown nosing. I proceeded to set up the plant and start pumping water. Meanwhile, the regular park men were removing the covers from the underwater lights.

I didn't have to change the lens this time because the assistant foreman changed them. I was pleased as that left me free to keep an eye on things inside the filter plant. I got a signal from Clarence, who was one of the regular men, to start pumping water whenever I was ready. I switched the pumps on and went up to see if the water was running into the pool. The water was flowing in the pool except through 5 or 6 injectors which were either blocked off or stopped up from charcoal that runs out of the bottom of the filters. As I was outside observing the water, the supervisor came over and he was still laughing and talking with this Tony character. They approached me and the boss said, "Mr. Brown I was talking to Tony here and I also talked to his father on the phone concerning the shift arrangements. Well, it appears that it had been arranged that he would work midnight to eight. I also found out that as supervisor, I can decide who works what shift, and besides, his old man's a friend of mine. We started out together as assistant gardeners."

Meanwhile, Tony just stood there sneering. Well if that didn't just take the cake. Neither of them noticed the black car pulling up in front of the building entrance as they were walking over. I saw a familiar well-dressed figure coming around the pool so I said, "well I'm sorry but I don't go along with that at all." The familiar figure approached us and said, "Good Morning Marvin, How are you doing?" I explained the situation to Mr. Joe Dee who was now Assistant Borough Director of Brooklyn and pulling a bit more weight. He informed the supervisor, Mr. Zeccia that Marvin Brown here has worked for the department a very long time. He is one of our best seasonal workers and as a number one man in the filter house at this facility. He has the responsibility of teaching these new fellows the job for which he receives no extra pay. I think the very least we can do for him is to allow him first choice of shifts. Mr. Zeccia began rocking and bowing and saluting as if he was talking to the president or a general. "Sure Joe . . . sure whatever you say." the supervisor turned to Tony and said, "You understand now Tony that Mr. Defazio here is my immediate superior."

Mr. Joe Dee to the rescue, Tony walked away with a sour expression on his face and cursing under his breath. Mr. Joe Dee went to look at the pool with the supervisor in tow clicking his heels and saluting all the way. Well, that settled that or did it? I reckoned I fixed his little red wagon good enough and now to get on with the business of running the filter house. I started to try and explain to Tony how the filter plant worked. But he didn't seem to be interested and was content to sit on the bleachers and read the horse race section of the newspaper and to fill out his betting sheets. I knew what I had to do.

By the end of the week, they sent down a third guy for the filter plant. He was a nice kid, named Larry, a college student and worked far more willingly than Tony. He wanted to know what shift he would be working so I told him it was between him and Tony to choose between 8 to 4 or 4 to 12, so he took the 8 to 4 and Tony took the 4 to 12 shift. I had the 12 to 8 shift. The following Monday, I started to work for Coleman Younger Motorcycle Messenger Service. We worked out of the film center building on 9th Avenue and 45th Street.

There were about ten guys including Fearless Dave and myself. We all rode different types of bikes. The job consisted of delivering film or TV commercials to all the TV stations and advertising agencies in the city, as well as delivering manuscripts and stage costumes. I was introduced to all the guys and given a receipt book that I was instructed to write down all the deliveries. The delivery charge was $3 per package. Coleman Younger was a cowboy from Texas and his father who was some big oil millionaire didn't get along with him and chased him away from home. He came to New York on his motorcycle and got a job as a messenger for a small messenger service. They realized the potential increase in business which could be done with motorcycle messengers. They hired a number of guys with motorcycles and then put Younger in charge of them. However, as the story was told, Younger was far more ambitious than the company realized. He thought, why, should I work so hard for them. He requested some money from his mother, who he was still on good terms with. He not only got out and formed his own company, but took with him the largest accounts and all the motorcycles messengers.

My first job was a trip to NBC with a roll of film for somebody named Geroge Bishoff. I remember that one because when I came out of the building, there was a cop writing a parking ticket to hang on my bike and there was a police tow truck standing there and two other cops trying to figure the best way of getting my bike onto the truck. Well, I was outraged and let it be known. I wanted to know why they were writing tickets for a poor hard working legitimate guy like me when there was so much crime going on. They informed me, in no uncertain terms that they were part of the Mayor's task force to rid the city streets of all illegally parked vehicles that were currently polluting the city. Motorcycles were included. Though I was allowed to take my bike and go, I was madder than a bag full of rattlesnakes. After all, I wasn't even in the building for ten minutes, and now I had a parking ticket for $15. I made on this first trip only $1.50. When I got back to the office, I explained the situation to Coleman Younger who was a very nice guy and said in his Texas drawl as he pushed back his cowboy hat and scratched his head, "Well Marv, I'm afraid there isn't too much I can do about that. That's happened to a couple of the fellows here and well, we try to take it with a grain of salt." He pointed to one guy who had walked into the office behind me. "Now, you take Ol Beeza Mike there, why he's done had his BSA towed away three times in the past month and I understand how you must feel and I'm sorry but it's like I said, you just can't fight City Hall."

Well, whether or not you could fight City Hall was a matter of opinion and I was going to figure out how to give them a run for their money. At that time, the phone rang and Cole was writing as he spoke to whoever was on the phone. When he hung up, he came over to me and said, "Marv, I'm going to let you earn that money back to pay for that ticket you got. I've got a trip out to the Eastman Kodak Labs in Fairlawn, New Jersey. There you'll pick up a roll of film, then keep on up to New Rochelle and make a pick up there. You'll then come back here with both packages. Now Marv, the Kodak job is worth $15 and the other thing is worth $10, but I'm not going to take one dime of that money because I want you to be happy here, especially as you are a friend of Dave's."

I expressed my gratitude and after receiving instructions on how to get there, I was on my way after stopping to fill my tank with Sunoco 260. After I made the New Jersey stop, I was on my way to New Rochelle when the clutch cable broke. However, I was ready for that as I had trouble with cables breaking before. I kept a spare of everything tucked away in the tool kit or head light and it only took me fifteen minutes to change it.

When I got back to the office, everybody was sitting around looking very unhappy. Fearless Dave related the story of Beeza

Mike who was on a delivery to East 57th Street. On his way back across 57th Street at Park Avenue, a driver, trying to make the light as he was traveling down Park Avenue, hit Mike broad-side at 50 mph. The impact was so great that it broke Mike's BSA into many pieces along with Mike's body. The cabbie claimed that he simply didn't see him and that was the end of Beeza Mike. I went home and made myself some dinner after which I lay across the bed for a quick nap and later rode out to the pool. When I arrived there, Tony was no where to be seen, and just as well as, we never had anything nice to say to each other anyway. He had obviously left a long time ago or had not been there at all, as the dry chemical feeders were empty and there was nothing written on the report pad from 4 to 12. The chlorine was running too high so I readjusted it and filled up everything. I rolled out my sleeping bag and went to sleep.

The next morning, I awoke at seven and looked out to see what I could see, and there on the other side of the pool, I could see the night watchman taking a stroll around the pool. Sometime back in January, I had made a list of all the skate guards and submitted it to the plumbing shops so that the skate guards who didn't work as life guards might have a chance to be filter plant operators. Bobby McDougal was one of the people on the list and he got appointed to work at Ham Fish Pool on the lower east side. I decided to stop down and see him and while I was visiting him, the water plant operators who service the pool were also there. I noticed that they had a couple of Park Dept. insignia stickers lying on the dash board of their pick-up truck. Since that was just what I needed, I decided to quickly liberate one of them while the operators were still inside the filter house.

When I arrived at the Film Center building, I pasted this sticker on the gas tank of my bike and when I came out of the NBC building later in the day, I found one cop looking at my gas tank and scratching his head probably trying to figure out when did the Park Dept. start using motorcycles. Oh well, if you can't beat them, join them. Anyway, I didn't get any more tickets.

The summer was a scorcher and dragged on at a snail's pace. The motorcycle messenger job was kind of fun sometimes and at other times it presented a few anxious moments. Like the time when a cab cut me off to make a right turn in front of me and as a natural reaction, I grabbed both brakes and slung the bike around so that I took a spill instead of going under the cab. The taxi driver didn't slow down, stop or look back. As far as cabbies are concerned, people on motorcycles don't exist. You're not there and therefore anybody riding a bike in New York City just has to be absolutely sharp and alert 100% of the time. Sensible bike riders who learn to ride in New York City and last for any number of years can certainly be regarded as the world's best motorcycle drivers. This is not by choice, but by necessity, if they want to keep on living. A motorcyclist must always drive defensibly. Whenever some eager beaver in a super car pulls up next to me at a traffic light and starts over-revving his engine to demonstrate how far in the gas tank he can shove his foot, when the light changes, I let him go first because I know he'll only leave tire tracks up my back and just keep going. The law says that a bike rider must keep in lane with the cars or one behind other motorcyclists. In my opinion, the worst thing a motorcyclist can do is drive behind a car. I formed this opinion from experience.

I have never run into anything, but I have been hit from behind or sandwiched between two cars a couple of times and as usual, the excuse is "I didn't see you!" People in cars think that they alone have exclusive use of the roads. Then there's the tin-head who thinks it is fun to drive his car up to within inches of a motorcyclist's rear fender or driving in front of a bike, stop short, just to see what the resulting reaction will be. Riding a bike is really great fun and gives you a feeling of real freedom. It would be even more fun upstate or in areas where there's more wide-open country than in New York City. I'm sure there are lots of other bike riders that feel the same way I do. If I were killed, people who knew me could truly say, "He died happy!"

When I'm riding on the Parkway, I always ride close to the edge of the lane so that I'm ready to respond on a half second's notice, whenever circumstances dictate. I can duck in between the two lanes or two cars ahead and get out of harm's way, I hope. Of course, when motorcyclists in the know ride that way, they should be well equipped with plenty of horse power, good brakes and a set of air horns that could stop a hungry-looking, penny-snatching cabdriver in his tire tracks. Most horns found on new bikes today don't have enough volume to frighten a pigeon. I have known guys to ride into New York City from other parts of the country and get wiped out just as soon as they get through the Lincoln Tunnel. Cab drivers just don't treat you right. Once you enter the city, it's a different type of riding.

After work, Fearless Dave and I would pick up a couple of girls that he knew and fill up our tanks with Sunoco 260 and ride up the New York State Throughway for a relaxing ride. Once when we were riding up the George Washington Bridge approach, there was a very sharp turn. Dave could never resist going around a turn at 90 mph. He took a spill as he was making the turn and it was a good thing he was riding alone. He was thrown off the bike and rolled and slid for 75 feet. He got up, picked up the bike, bump started it and kept on going. Although he is a little chubby, he is a tough little guy. You could throw him off the Empire State Building and he would bounce up and keep going.

The summer rolled on and Greg came home from basic training in Fort Gordon, Georgia. We got together whenever I could find the time so that he could ride my new bike. When I arrived at work, Tony usually wasn't at the plant. The chlorine tank would be empty and so would the dry chemical feeders. The weather was too hot to sleep, so all I could do was sit there and melt and listen to the whine of the pumps. One night when I came into work, I noticed it was unusually quiet, that is to say, the pumps weren't running. So I knew right away there was something wrong. Under normal operations, the filter plant has a certain and definite sound. The pumps have a unique sound, the dry chemical feeders have a unique sound and running water has a special sound. All these sounds together create a certain harmony and anytime one of these sounds is missing, the harmony is altered. Water spilling over the wall onto the floor from the top of the filters was a very dominating sound. Whenever I hear an unusual sound, I go down to investigate.

This time, I started down to investigate but I didn't get far down the stairs when all kinds of things came floating up. As usual, Tony was nowhere to be seen. As the deck lights were shorted out, I couldn't see that as I came in the gate, half of the water wasn't in the pool. The pool holds around one and a half million gallons of water. Half of the pool's water was down on the floor of the filter plant. The water level mark on the wall of the plant was around 9 feet high. It was the first and biggest flood that I had ever seen. The pumps and all electric equipment were under water and short-circuited. I climbed over the pipes to the cat walk to try and determined the reason for what went wrong. Before I even got to the cat walk, I could see that the basin level valve was stuck in an open position which meant that there was so much rust and grime accumulated in the valve and shaft housing that the whole thing couldn't function freely.

The pool uses a gravity system that works through a hydraulic arrangement where the water pressure is balanced with the help of a counter weights hanging from a cable and controlled by a bucket of water. The bucket has a float inside that moves up or down whenever the amount of water in the bucket is increased or decreased. The water enters the bucket through a pipe that is connected through the influent valve of the filter at the far end of the cat walk. When that filter has taken in enough water to bring it sufficiently level, the bucket which is at the same level as that filter receives its share of water. This makes the float rise and directs the water pressure through the top of the hydraulic valve, forcing it to close, reducing the amount of water running down to the filters. The pools were all built during the depression by the WPA and all the older pools use this system. I prefer to work with this system rather than the new push button pressure systems that are being installed now.

I personally think the gravity system is a very good system when kept properly maintained by the shops. The machinists from Five Borough Shops are supposed to dismount these valves, floats and the filters which no longer turn freely during the winter and clean out all foreign matter. At the end of the season, I make out a list of things to be repaired in the filter plant during the winter and submit it to the shops. I have submitted this repair list for the pool for years and nothing was ever done about it. They never do anything because the City never hires people that aren't afraid to do a days work. They only hire people who want to get paid for a day's work without doing a day's work.

As this valve opened all the way and froze, the water from the pool just continued to run into the filters and poured over the top and onto the floor until the water on the floor reached the same level with the water in the pool. There wasn't much I could do about it now. It was just too late. I went across to the office to sign in and inform the night watchman of the situation in order to clear myself of the blame. There was no need of calling the shops at 12 midnight, as there wouldn't be anybody there, anyway. I knew that the Fire Dept. was used in major floods to pump out the water, so I called them. A lieutenant came and took a look and informed me that he couldn't very well order a pump down here that might be badly needed somewhere else and that while they were down here pumping out the filter plant, ten houses could burn down. He then got in his car and disappeared. I agreed with him on that.

I almost had a flood myself once because of that sticking float. I managed to catch it in time, by racing up the cat walk ladder and closing all the influent valves at the filters. I called the shop at 8 a.m. the next day and hung around while they made the repairs. When the supervisor came in, he came over and started down the stairs. He grabbed the railing with his left hand and with the right hand up to his head, he fell backwards exclaiming, "Oh my God!" Good thing I was standing behind him and caught him or he would have fallen on the floor. Pretty soon the shops came, including the electricians, the plumbers and the water plant operators and machinists. Also a few important people from the Arsenal and the Brooklyn Borough Office came. When I left for my other job, they were buzzing around like bees in a hive. I made a suggestion as to how floods might be avoided but as I'm only a seasonal, no one even listened to me. I believe that if two pumps of the same type used to pump out the sump tank could be installed at about 8 feet off the floor, with the intakes built below floor level, and switch operated, the small sump pump could resolve the problem. When this smaller pump is submerged in a flood, the larger pumps can go into action. The flood could be cleared up and the equipment repaired and put back into operation quickly.

Tony's father used his influence to prevent Tony from getting fired because of the flooding. On Labor Day, the pool season came to an end. After a number of trips out to the GHOST Dealership to get my bike fixed, because a car had backed up and knocked it over or some truck driver had backed up on top of it, requiring the replacement of a new front end. I figured the money I made from Coleman Younger wasn't sufficient to pay for all the repairs and the trouble I had to deal with my bike, so I cut him loose. Big Rick called me at home from the rink to say that I should go to the Arsenal and get reappointed, as it was time to make ice. Opening day came and my crew was pretty much made up of the same guys I had the previous season. Mr. Joe Dee wasn't there any more, as he had gone on to bigger and better things. I believe they said, he was the safety commissioner with his offices in Flushing Meadows and his job was to hold safety meetings with all the supervisors. The supervisor was Mr. Lagonick who was only going to be there long enough for his transfer to come through. He was supposed to get an easy job on a golf course somewhere. Meanwhile, he didn't take too much interest in Wollman and was a poor substitute for Mr. Joe Dee.

The Arsenal appointed some new foremen and one of them was a former fingerprint man from the personnel office, Mr. Bill Challender. My first impression of him with his big eyes, big mouth and large forehead, was that he was a no nonsense, and I mean right this minute, type of foreman. He could scare the hell out of a skate guard in a minute. I immediately pegged him as being another Joe Dee. I personally think they should have made him supervisor right then. But on the other hand, he was new to the rink operation and there's the question of seniority.

CHAPTER VI

This morning, Connie told me that she thought it best that we go our separate ways, as she was still in school and planned to be a teacher when she finished. The last time I saw her, her parting words were, "I love you Marv, but I don't like you!" That left me with a problem to solve. What was she talking about? If she loved me, she must like me and how could she love me without liking me in the first place. It just didn't make sense to me and if she did love me, what was she leaving me for? Well, I know we had our disagreements occasionally. After all she was a Leo and I was a Scorpio and as fire and water don't blend too well, we would naturally disagree sometimes. But I never had any idea it would end like this or if indeed it would end at all. Just the same, we parted as friends and I still consider her one of the warmest and gentlest person I've known.

The season moved along and the crew functioned like clockwork. The supervisor spent most of his time sitting in the office smoking a cigar with his feet up on the desk. He didn't care much about what went on outside his office. It snowed for the first time on Thanksgiving Day and after I had all the snow piled at the rear of the ice, I went into the office to ask the supervisor if he could request a frontend loader to come down from Randall's Island or 79th Street Yard to carry out the snow. He only leaned back in his chair to make himself more comfortable, took a couple of good puffs from his cigar and said, "To hell with that snow." Well needless to say, I was quite shocked, not at the profane remark which I hear in the locker room all day long, but at the obvious unconcern of a man who was assigned here to supervise and oversee all operations. But then on the other hand, I started working here when there were supervisors like Ginkiller and Joe Dee and was conditioned and deceived into thinking that all future supervisors would operate along the same principles and interests as they did. Meanwhile, the new fingerprint foreman from the Arsenal was really buzzing around enthusiastically and really getting involved in everything. One day, I was short of help and didn't have anybody to drive the jeep. Mr. Callender, though he was the foreman, pitched right in and lent a helping hand by driving the cut.

One day immediately after finishing the cut, I was called into the office. Upon entering, I saw a heavy set white haired man, in a park supervisor's uniform, sitting behind the desk. The supervisor and a visiting supervisor were standing. Mr. Brown, said the man sitting behind the desk, "My name is Mr. Jones, I'm the Assistant Borough Director of Manhattan." I'm here because I have a sad duty to perform, and it has everything to do with you. Mr. Sam Sleight who is the Director of Maintenance and Operations has warned you repeatedly against parking your motorcycle in the park. He has now decided that his words of warning was cast on deaf ears and has ordered me to come here and take necessary measures against you. Mr. Brown as of this moment, you're no longer employed by the Department of Parks. You're fired." He then rose from the chair and walked out.

Well, if that ain't the last straw. I was literally dumbfounded. I didn't know what to do. Sure somebody said, "You really shouldn't park your bike there, it's against the law." But I considered it a matter for the police dept. or the cop that was stationed at the rink. Besides, I had heeded those warnings and left my bike parked out on 64ᵗʰ Street in front of the Arsenal where it was promptly knocked over by a diplomat's car in front of the Indian Embassy. I always found my bike lying on its side or flung up on the sidewalk with the fenders and tank bent or the front end out of alignment. This happened so often, it didn't pay to even have the bike fixed. So I figured I'd better put it where I knew it would be safe. Anyway, half the personnel at Wollman had their cars parked up on the grass just outside the rink. So, I didn't see why I couldn't park my bike, which took up much less space, under a bush in an obscure corner, where no one ever walked or even noticed. Sam Sleight, a man whose name I had never heard unless it was in connection with having somebody being brought up on charges, disciplined or fired, had now sent down his hatchet man to do his dirty work.

Sam Sleight, the man who runs the department, was the third man in the hierarchy of power. Counting from the top down, or to put it another way, first comes the Commissioner, second his Deputy and third the Director of Maintenance and Operations. He is responsibility for 37,000 acres of parkland and thousands of employees. This means that his power is almost absolute and whatever he says goes, without question or challenge, especially, not from some lowly seasonal worker. Well, Mr. Sam Sleight, you don't know who you're messing with, and you have a fight on your hands. I ain't about to take this standing up or lying down or any other kind of way. FIRE ME, from the place where I shed much of my own blood to ensure that the sessions started on time. FIRE ME, from this place where I spent more time working my ass off than I spent at home. FIRE ME, from this place, where for the first time in my life, I was given authority, as small as it was, stimulating all of my hidden ambitions and raising in me, a desire for even more power. FIRE ME, from this place that I love so much. FIRE ME, I don't think so. Did he really think that I could be just brushed away like the dandruff on his lapel of his fancy tweed jacket? Did he think I was afraid of him, just because he was a big shot in the Parks Dept and I was but a lowly skate guard who slid around over the ice at Wollman Rink, like a worm crawls over a fallen leaf. Is that what he thought? Well, I've got news for him.

I felt tears well up in my eyes as my entire being started to tremble. The anger and confusion that boiled and dripped from this new wound, so carelessly inflicted against the depths of my freshly torn soul. My knees weakened and I had to lean against a wall to support myself from fainting. Mr. Viola was one of the foremen. He said to me, "I'm going up and have a word with the Borough Director about this matter. Meanwhile, you'd better go and have a talk with your rabbi and I hope you have a good one, 'cause that's what it's going to take to deal with this man. Nobody likes him!" A good rabbi! I wasn't even Jewish. I took my bike and went home and went to bed even though it was only three o'clock when I got home. As I was tired, I fell into a deep sleep and when I woke up, it was midnight. I lay awake the rest of the night trying to figure out what to do. I came to the conclusion that the only way to get around Sam Sleight was to go over his head, directly to the Commissioner. After all, I was probably the first skate guard he ever met and shook hands with. Maybe he'll remember who I was. He also rode a bike. He had a 305 Honda which caught fire one day when he was riding down 5th Avenue.

If anybody could give me my job back, it would have to be Mr. Hoving. I got out of bed at 5 a.m. and looked in the phone book to see if he was listed and sure enough, his name was there. He lived on East 73rd Street, off Park Avenue.

So at 6 a.m., I got on my bike and rode over there. I had no idea when he would be leaving his house to go to the Arsenal. But I knew that a black limousine with a park leaf shield on the back would come for him. At 6:30, I was there and waiting in front of the building. At 7:00 sharp, his car came and two minutes later he came out the door and walked toward his car, very fast. I approached him and said, "Mr. Hoving, may I speak to you for a moment sir?" He cast a rather shocked look in my direction and said in a very gruff voice, "NO" and without even breaking his stride, continued to his car and got in and rode away. It wasn't the kind of reaction I was prepared for and didn't expect that at all.

Well, what to do next was the question. I decided the best thing to do was to go on up to the Arsenal and try to see him there at his office, even if I had to make a nuisance of myself. The Arsenal's third floor doesn't start functioning until 9 o'clock. This made me wonder why the Commissioner left home so early. I decided to have coffee in the zoo cafeteria and wait until 9 o'clock. Would you believe that that sanctimonious Mr. Sam Sleight came in and sat at the very next table to drink his coffee? Well, I just kept giving him the meanest look I had. He didn't know who I was, but I must have frightened him because he got up and left.

Promptly at 9 o'clock, I went up to the third floor of the Arsenal and asked the receptionist if I could possibly see the

Commissioner. She informed me that the Commissioner wasn't in his office this morning. However, if I would have a seat, his secretary would like to talk to me as soon as she found the time. After about ten minutes, the secretary came out and I explained to her my situation. She replied that she thought Mr. Sleight's action was rather extreme and unnecessary and at the most he should have sent a policeman to write me a ticket. She said, that yes, she would speak to Mr. Hoving about this. Well, I went away feeling rather satisfied and with more peace of mind than I had in a couple of days since the events took place. It really seemed like a couple of years. It was Thursday and of course, I didn't hesitate to stop down at Wollman's to tell the crew to get ready for the grand return of their great chief. Afterwards, I went home feeling rather satisfied.

On Saturday, the phone rang around noon and it was the Commissioner. He said, "Mr. Brown, I heard what happened to you and I'm sorry I didn't have time to talk to you the other morning, but I was in a hurry to go to a conference with The Mayor of New York City."

Well, I thought he doesn't have to explain to me, I know he's a very busy person. All he has to say is that I've got my job back and everything is back to status quo. However, that's not at all what he said. I just wasn't ready for what he did say. We're opening up Lasker Rink in two weeks and we're going to need a good ice chief and skate guards up there. Report to the Borough Director's Office on Monday and he'll have you reinstated. At those words, I was dazed even more. I don't know what he said after that or if he said anything at all. The tears welled up in my eyes and I just couldn't figure out what to do. My attention wandered back to the phone. Somebody was calling my name. "Mr. Brown, Mr. Brown are you still there? Mr. Brown did you understand what I've just said?" "Oh yes, yes I understand. Thank you very much sir! I'll go in and see the Borough Director on Monday. Thank you. Good bye."

Sure, I knew they had a new rink under construction at the north end of Central Park at 110th Street. I had passed it many times when I rode around the park on my bike. But I never had the remotest idea that it would touch my life in any way, nor had I ever inquired about it. Al Erber had once told me that Lasker Rink was to be a swimming pool and ice rink combined and that it was the second one ever built in the world with the first one being built in Japan. Other than that, I had no other knowledge about it, nor was I interested in it, being perfectly content at Wollman. Monday morning at 9 o'clock, I entered the Arsenal and started down the hall toward the Borough Director's office. A slim white-haired man came running out of his office and met me half way up the hall, shaking my hand and asking, "Is your name Brown?" Before I could answer, "You are Brown! Come into my office." He took me by the hand and half dragged me down the hall and into his office. "Brown, the Commissioner wants to know the minute you got here. I must ring him up. "He dialed three numbers and somebody on the other end answered the phone and started to talk. The Borough Director nodded a couple of times as he said, "Yes sir, I understand." He hung up the phone and took a deep breath, leaned back in his chair, twined his finger together and said, "The Commissioner told me to talk to you like a Dutch uncle ... and ... well frankly, I don't know what

I should say to you. Except that, if you were told to keep your motorcycle out of the park you should have done that. Well, Mr. Viola has told me what a good man you are. You've really got the Arsenal in quite an uproar. Mr. Sleight is upset because you went over his head. Well, I wouldn't want you to get fired. After all, good men are hard to come by. You'll start to work up at Lasker the day after tomorrow and I think there's a place where you can park your motorcycle. You can go downstairs to personnel and be reappointed." So, I went downstairs to go through the ritual of forms and fingerprints. After the forms, I had to go back upstairs and sit on the bench outside Mr. Veackie's office and wait while he darted in and out of offices up and down the hall, conversing with anybody and everybody. It seemed to me that he was doing nothing, just creating the appearance of doing work.

This was the only thing I disliked about getting appointed was waiting for hours outside of Mr. Veakie's office, when all he had to do was write my name in a book, give me a button with a number on it and let me sign my name in a different book. All this took less than three minutes. Meanwhile, I had to wait and wait and wait.

Mr. Veakie should retire and let a younger man take over. I'm sure he has made enough money. I'll bet he's been here since year one. A week ago, I received a citation in the mail from the New York State Department of Motor vehicles. It was about that speeding ticket I received earlier in the summer. It requested an appearance tomorrow in court, in a town called Mineola, on Long Island. I figured the best way to get to Mineola was to take the train. So, bright and early the next morning, I was at the Long Island railroad terminal buying a round trip ticket to Mineola. I took the train and arrived at Mineola in about an hour. I walked from the train station toward the center of town. After asking around, I finally located the court building. I was a couple of hours early but decided I would enter and observe the proceedings against the other traffic violators. One woman who had received a parking ticket was complaining that she had always left her car parked on the street in front of her house as she didn't have a driveway. The young cop on the beat didn't understand that he was not supposed to write her up.

The judge who really looked very bored said, "Madam. Your car was illegally parked and should have been ticketed, whether by a young cop or an old one, fined $10, Next case!" The next case was a man who had already been to court two weeks earlier on a drunken driver charge. He had been fined $50 or 30 days in jail. Since he didn't have the $50, he was given two weeks to get the money. However, after two weeks, he still didn't have the money. The judge unmercifully, ordered the correction officers to take him away.

A door opened toward the rear of the court room and a policeman entered, bent forward under the burden of what looked to me like chains. As he entered, I could see that indeed they were chains and attached to them at the other end were 8 other men, each one chained to the other by hand and by foot. They were dragged in and roughly shoved into a corner where they sat down on a bench. I don't know what they had done but it sure must have been something bad. I began to conjure up in my mind a picture of myself being dragged in on the end of a chain after the police had arrested me at my home. Boy, I was glad I came in as requested. When my turn came, the judge called my name and said, "Mr. Brown, you were caught doing 60 in a 50 zone. How do you plea?" Well, how did he think I was going to plea? I most certainly couldn't afford to spend a lot of money in court costs just to prove I wasn't guilty of speeding, when he would most likely believe the cop anyway. So, I naturally said, "Guilty as charged!" "That'll be a $10 fine. Pay the Bailiff!"

When I got back to the city, I stopped at Wollman's to see the boys and inform them of the latest developments. I learned that they had gone through three ice chiefs in as many days before they finally came up with what they thought was a suitable subject. On Wednesday, I reported to the supervisor at Lasker Rink who turned out to be the visiting supervisor that was in the office at Wollmans on the day I got fired.

Mr. Bookbinder was his name. He was short and appeared to be a very amiable fellow and we really got along quite well. He had been at Wollmans observing the operation on that fateful day. Lasker Rink was a shiny new structure, built of stone, steel, glass and aluminum. Lasker Rink, originally planned by Lula Lasker who donated the money for its construction, was to be a swimming pool. However, some genius downtown somewhere had gotten the bright idea and told them to run refrigeration coils under it and call it a skating rink as well. Lasker Rink was later to be referred to within the department as the city's "white elephant." Well, white elephant or Lulu or whatever it was called, I was stuck with it. After all I had to work someplace and I guess this was as good a place as any, even if I felt like I had been thrown into the briar patch.

When I first walked into the place, it was spilling over with workers from the Dept. of Parks. They were involved in laying rubber mats all over the place. Half the mats were later taken up and sent down to Wollman. The Lasker Rink was called "Rink." Although it was so named, from all outward appearances, it looked to me like a swimming pool into which someone had built two ramps from the deck down onto the floor of the pool—one ramp on either side of the pool.

Four motor vehicle operators were involved in piling and loading snow onto a dump truck which was driven out, up the ramp and down to the lake where it was then dumped. Mr. Bookbinder informed me that I would have to choose the skate guards and two chiefs, organize and train them and teach the new chiefs how to process the ice. He had already hired a few seasonal workers whom he had working for him during the summer. Later in the morning, two skate guards came up from Wollman. They said they were transferred to the Rink after they answered a request from the Borough Director for two guys that could serve as chiefs. They had both been on my crew at Wollman: Mike Franquez and Joe Rivera. Mr. Bookbinder told them to report to me for instructions.

The first thing I had to do was organize the guys that had been hired and get the floor of the pool or should I say, get the slab cleaned. When we went out to the pool/rink, I had not yet decided who would be the receptionist to answer the telephone at the rink, especially as the people in the office answered the phone by saying Lasker Pool. I wanted to help the motor vehicle operators (MVOs) with the snow removal equipment. However, one particular MVO had lost one of the chains from the rear wheel of the tractor which he was operating and he decided that we lowly seasonal workers should find it and replace it. I took pleasure in informing him that as he was operating the tractor and he was getting $10,000 a year, he would be the one to replace the chain when it was repaired. He was just another Dept. of Parks worker who was trying to give seasonal workers a hard way to go.

They ran the refrigeration plant for the past week to make sure everything was functioning properly. Because of this, much of the snow had been frozen onto the slab and we had to spend the rest of the day cutting away the snow and ice that had formed. And as they didn't have a pit like at Wollman, I had to operate the front end loader to carry away the snow. By the end of the day when I got home, I was dead tired. As I was watching the 11 o'clock news, there was a news report and a film showing us cutting away and carrying out the snow earlier in the day. They said something about the rink being scheduled to open next week.

That night, I went to sleep and dreamed of ice, miles and miles of ice. The next day when I arrived at work, I got the boys organized and pulled out the hose to get on with the business of washing down the slab. But I found the hose frozen solid. It was understandable, especially as the hose had been built onto the edge of the deck outside in the open. The hose at Wollman's is kept inside the building for that very reason. We spent a couple of hours carrying buckets full of hot water to pour over the hose. When it was thawed enough to use, we proceeded with the job at hand. I sprayed the water over the slab and the guys pushed it off with brooms and squeegees. Only trouble was, the water had no place to drain off and it just ran back onto the slab. There was one drain somewhere in a corner of the pool and all I had to do was find where it was. I don't know who was responsible for building that place, but I have a feeling that he didn't ask anybody anything about how an ice rink should be built or requirements of a rink. We found out where the drain was and then fought like hell to keep that tidal wave moving in the right direction. After I was satisfied that the slab was clean enough, I asked the supervisor where they kept the white wash and he said, "What white wash? What do you need that for?" I explained what white wash was used for, after which he got on the phone to the Arsenal and talked to Mr. Gilligan who worked out of Sam Sleight's office. After he hung up the phone, he said that, "Sam Sleight said we aren't to use any white wash because he didn't think we needed it."

Well, I assured him that we did need it, if the ice was to hold properly on warm days. On my way out, I met Mr. Callender who had been sent up to lend a hand and his first words after saying hello was, "Say Marv, when are you going to white wash?"

I explained what Mr. Sam Sleight had said. As far as I was concerned, Sam Sleight was continually presenting himself as a stumbling block in my path. If I made ice on top of this pool paint and the sun came out and melted it away, Mr. Sleight, without a doubt, would be the very first one to point a finger at me as being irresponsible, incompetent and untrustworthy. He would then try to fire me again. While in the tool shed, I noticed a large canvas thrown over a stack of sacks. I pulled it away to discover 20 bags of white wash. Well, I had the white wash and I'm going to white wash the slab, no matter what Mr. Sam Sleight said. Anyway, he's down there and I'm up here. The supervisor went home and left me and the boys to make ice after sundown. I ordered the crew to bring out the white wash and I found a fifty gallon drum. We mixed it up and spread it over the slab. The refrigeration plant was put into operation by the engineer and the minute a frost showed over the slab I started spraying. We worked all night and by morning, we had built about two inches of ice. When the supervisor arrived in the morning, he was quite satisfied with our work.

At 9 o'clock, a black car pulled up outside the gate and a tall man got out and came inside. He walked down the ramp onto the ice, across the ice and up the ramp on the other side and into the building. Well, there he was, Mr. Sam Sleight, dressed in his black and white checkered pants, black and white checkered shoes and he had black and white checkered eyeballs. Two minutes after he entered the building, there came such a shouting and screaming like I never heard before. After the shouting stopped, Mr. Sam Sleight came out and walked quickly toward his chauffeured car, giving me a dirty look as he passed. The feeling was mutual.

I was busy checking the oil and water and gassing up the equipment. The supervisor came out immediately after, looking very sullen and still smarting from the tongue lashing he received. He said, "Sam Sleight said that the ice is going to slide off the slab!" "What a ridiculously dumb statement for a supposedly intelligent person to make," I said. "Well, I don't know," said the boss. "He said that when he walked across it, it cracked under his weight." You will never meet a more ignorant person, than an educated fool.

"Of course it cracks," I said. "Whenever you spray water on it and the water freezes, it will expand and because it expands when it freezes, the ice will crack when you walk or skate across it!" "Well, I don't know," said the supervisor. "He has the biggest job, so he's supposed to know." "Well, that just shows how much he doesn't know about ice," I said. "Can you just imagine, 2800 square feet of ice becoming unattached from the slab and sliding off across the park. I wonder how he wangled his way into that job anyway. "The supervisor just laughed. He always laughed at everything.

The crews were chosen, Joe and Mike were put on chief's pay and the two of them together were to work nights. I had been having trouble getting up the ramp with the front end loader under a load of snow because the steel wire mesh used for traction wasn't properly nailed down or because there wasn't any nails long enough to hold it. So, I repeatedly asked the supervisor for these and other things that we needed, such as chain pliers and bolt cutters. The supervisor repeatedly sent in requisitions for supplies to Mr. Gilligan, with no results. During the dedication ceremony, the Mayor came with his people from City Hall and the Commissioner with a lot of other people from the Arsenal. There was a lot of fancy talk and dedication speeches and hand clapping. After the speeches, the Mayor and Commissioner and a few other people laced on their skates to do a bit of skating and test out the new ice. I must say that the Mayor cut quite a step on his figure skates. I gather he was a mustard cutter from way back.

However, the Commissioner didn't go in for any of that fancy stuff, as he was skating on rented hockey skates. Mr. Gilligan, who was responsible for filling our requests for the things we needed to run the place, was walking around inspecting the rink. When the Commissioner finally skated off the ice and came close enough to me so I could have a word with him, I told him about all the things we needed and why we needed them and we couldn't get them. He went over to Gilligan and started screaming and pointing his finger. Later, after the Commissioner and the Mayor and all their people left, Gilligan came over and said, "You skate guards should never talk to the Commissioner. You're just not allowed to do that. He then left. As far as I am concerned, the end justified the means. If I must speak to the man at the top to get results, then I'll speak to him without hesitation. I don't care if others may not like it.

CHAPTER VII

A couple of days later, we received everything. We received not only one bolt cutter but two, plus a large carton full of nails of every size and shape in the catalogue. It was said that we could get anything we wanted. So, I put in a requisition for a jeep for each chief. But of course, they turned that down.

Opening day came and went. Although the crowds were somewhat moderate on weekends, during the week there were only 2 or 3 people in the morning and 3 or 4 in the afternoon. The ten skate guards on duty harassed the skaters and even they left. They gave us a machine which was supposed to cut ice, called a rink master. However, it did not function as it was supposed to. Later, I learned that the city bought it for $11,000 in order to keep from buying a $18,000 Zamboni machine which is a better machine. Even though it stays in the shop half the time, it prepares the ice quite well, when it works.

The Rink Master turned out to be such a flop with its dragging sacks and bags. We ended up using it to pull the cutter. For the money they spent for that thing, they could have bought two jeeps which were exactly what I would have wanted for the ice. The Rink Master reminded me of a creation that Mr. Joe Dee conceived and Frank Dolittle developed. It consisted of a water tank sitting in the back of the jeep with a water pipe running down to the ice covered with a burlap bag through which the water was spread over the ice. Two skate guards had to skate along behind it and keep it from freezing onto the ice when the jeep stopped. Dolittle named it "The Defazioni of Wollman." And I must say, in all fairness, it worked better than the Rink Master which was a waste of taxpayer's money. I believe it's currently in service out at the Flushing Rink, pulling the cutter around. I wish the people who bought this equipment, before they go out and spend more taxpayer's money; they should talk to us first.

I would have preferred two fully equipped Jeeps or scouts. They can keep the Rink Masters and Zambonies which are built for small indoor rinks and are ineffective in a snow storm anyway. The only tools needed by a good chief, are two Jeeps, a crew of good men and a good supervisor to back him up.

A couple of days after opening day, Mr. Sam Sleight paid us another call. This time, he was rather calm. Instead of yelling at the supervisor, he complimented him on doing a good job and said something about how pleased the Commissioner was. Now, here is a man who was notorious throughout the Parks Dept. for showing up at a park facility half an hour before quitting time bringing a camera and a clock. He would place the clock next to a blotter where someone had signed out half an hour too early and would photograph the blotter and clock together showing the difference in the actual time and the time on a blotter. He would then bring this person or persons up on charges, using this photograph as evidence. I don't see where that's valid evidence as he could fix the clock to show whatever time he wanted it to show. As a result, these people are fined a week's pay or fired outright. And now, after the Commissioner had been there, looked the place over and liked what he saw, this guy Sleight, who probably never had an original idea in his entire life, is most likely figuring out ways to keep his job and keep the Commissioner happy. Well, Sam Sleight can just take two big running jumps and go to hell.

One day, I received a call from Frenchie who was the night chief at the Wollman Rink. He informed me that all the skate guards in all the rinks were to walk off the job at 3:30 p.m. and go on strike. I was to take my guys and meet everyone at City Hall where we are supposed to demonstrate. We all got together at City Hall where there was supposed to be a Christmas tree lighting ceremony on the steps. The Mayor was supposed to officiate while we walked around making a lot of noise and carrying signs that read "down with the Mayor, down with the Arsenal, down with the Commissioner and up with the skate guards and up with the money!"

The Mayor came out and went through some kind of tree lighting ceremony wishing peace on earth and good will to all men, and then, he threw the switch. Nothing happened. The tree didn't light because one of the skate guards had cut the wire. I still don't know whether that was in the demonstration plans or not. We later went up to demonstrate in front of the Arsenal where the guys from the Brooklyn rinks were very angry. Especially, as the Brooklyn Borough Director tried to fire one of the chiefs because he felt that his chief was the cause of the strike.

We demonstrated in front of the Arsenal. I didn't see that this was doing any good, since there was no one in the Arsenal after 5 p.m., except maybe, a night watchman. He was probably asleep since it was after 8 o'clock p.m. Anyway, a union representative showed up and told us that what we were doing was not legal. It was a wild cat strike and that we didn't have the union's support. Many of the guys, especially the ones from Brooklyn, told him that the union had never done anything for them anyway. And indeed they hadn't to my knowledge. They then demanded to know what he was doing coming here interfering with the strike in the first place. Just whose side was he on and who was it in the Arsenal that was paying him off. Somebody said "Let's drag him around behind the Arsenal and throw him in the seal pool." At that time, the union rep tried to make his exit. They grabbed him and dragged him screaming and kicking off to the seal pool.

After all was said and done, we received a pay increase of $5 more per day for chiefs and $3 more per day for skate guards. This was retroactive for two years. In addition, there was also an increase for my pool job under the same conditions. The union promptly stepped forward to claim all the credit for the pay increases and everybody knew that they had nothing to do with it.

Although our pay increase wasn't to go into effect for a couple of months, everyone returned to work temporarily satisfied. On Christmas Eve, it started snowing. I asked the guys on both crews if they wanted to stay overnight and make some T.C.(time coming). They did and we spent the whole night battling snow. While engaged in moving the snow the next morning with the front end loader, two of my guys, Robert and Effrin Soto, called my attention to what looked liked two hands sticking up out of a snow drift close to the outside of the fence. Indeed, there were two hands sticking through the snow and a face too. I informed the boss who called the Police Dept. When they removed the body, there was an empty wine bottle lying nearby. Some poor soul had gotten drunk and laid down or fallen down in all that snow and froze to death. "God rest his soul, whoever he was."

On one occasion, a couple of guys came up from Wollman and said they would rather work for me than work for the chief down there, whoever he was. I didn't know it at the time, but these guys had been fired by Mr. Callender. Not knowing this, I told the boss to send them to the officer for rink appointments. One of them, Pete O'Done, took the front end loader on a very snowy night and went joy riding through the park towards Wollman. There he managed to get the tractor stuck in the snow near the Zoo. The foreman who was working the snow watch at Wollman that night, offered to have his guys pull him out with the Jeep, if he, Pete O'Done, would allow them at Wollman to use the machine to clear their rink, which they did. By the time O'Done got back up to Lasker, it was after 8 a.m. and the supervisor was on duty. Brian, who was one of the chiefs at Wollman had managed to break some of the hydraulic lines on the tractor which we needed to move our own snow. The foreman at Wollman denied he ever saw Pete or the tractor and that he knew absolutely nothing about nothing. Pete was fired permanently. There were a lot of angry people at the Arsenal and at the shops too. There is the old story of skate guards in uniform on tractors drag racing across 42nd Street in the middle of the night. I dare say, a skate guard leads an exciting life, never a dull moment.

Then, there was the day when a few of the younger skate guards thought it was fun to play on the tractor, by starting and gassing the engine. Well, during the course of this playing, one guy took his turn at the tractor and started it, gassed it and accidently threw it into gear. The tractor which had a snow plow on the front was parked on the deck of the pool/rink behind a guard rail. He sped forward, knocking down the rail, the hose, ripping up the pipes and finally came to rest with one wheel hanging off the deck over the pool/rink. The skate guard then jumped off the tractor and ran to the locker room, climbed into his locker and told the boys to close the locker door and hide him. Somebody thought it would be a good idea to take the locker with him in it down to the lake and throw it in.

Needless to say, somebody could have gotten hurt. After this incident, skate guards were no longer permitted to touch the equipment, only MVOs and chiefs. It was decided that Mike Franquez, who had developed a reputation for being a phantom chief. The supervisor could never find Mike. He was never there, despite the fact his name was always on the sign-in blotter. So, he was fired. I picked Effrin Soto, who I thought was the best man on my crew to replace him. He learned to box, cut and spray the ice, was always at work when he was supposed to be and very willing to work. I hung around late one evening to observe how the night crew worked. I was now a super chief. A title that did not exist and one in which I didn't receive extra money. Joe Rivera, who was the night chief, walked around giving orders like a regular army general. He carried the blotter under his arm and a pencil behind his ear, looking for the first sign of an insubordinate skate guard who he was ready to sign out. While I was there someone was injured. A skate guard blew the whistle for a stretcher. Somebody came with the stretcher and they loaded the injured person onto it. I said loaded because this guy must have weighed three hundred pounds. He was short and round. Anyway, the four skate guards picked up the stretcher and started up the ramp. One skate guard, Little Guy, because of his size, wasn't too steady on his feet. Little Guy, carrying one of the rear or lower ends of the stretcher, tripped and fell, dropping his corner of the stretcher. The injured man rolled off the stretcher, down the ramp, almost back onto the ice. He then jumped up and ran away. The skate guards ran after him and the crowd died laughing. What a circus at this Lulu Rink!

One evening as it was starting to rain, I thought I would stick around the rink/pool a while, as I had nothing to do when I got home anyway. The rain increased as night fell. It really started to come down. The facility was built over a stream that drains water into the lake from the upper part of the park. This stream ran under the facility from a ditch that ended in the parking lot in back of the building. The water ran into the drain pipe and ran under the building. There was a grate or catch basin to pick up the leaves and other trash that travels with the running water. As the night wore on and the rain increased, the catch basin became clogged up, stopping the flow of water. Having no place to go, the water filled up the ditch and the parking lot. There is a wall, with steps over it that is supposed to keep water from going into the building. However, after the water had filled up the parking lot and continued to rise, it finally poured over the wall and into the refrigeration plant. The engineer came charging up the stairs screaming, "HELP, HELP, HELP, it's a flood, the water broke down the door! Save my locker!"

And sure enough there was six feet of water down in the refrigeration plant. There was a manhole cover out in the parking lot which was supposed to be opened whenever the water looked threatening. Only the night watchman, who was supposed to do this, had stepped out to look for a friend. When he returned, he was walking around in the parking lot in water up to his chest, looking for the manhole cover. He never found it. Anyway, it was already too late. So now, every time it rains heavily, the engineer goes into a panic. I can't help but think that if Mrs. Lulu D. Lasker ever found out about all these things, she would have somebody's head on a chopping block or demand her money back and her name taken down. I wouldn't blame her either.

One Friday, Mr. Bookbinder told me to drive Mrs. Radcliff, who was our time keeper, down to the Arsenal to pick up our paychecks. While we were in the building, I ran into the Borough Director who greeted me and after telling me what a good job I had done in helping to get the place organized and into operation. He said, "We are going to close Lasker very soon and then you can come back down to Wollman for the remaining part of the season. After all, I think you've been sent to Siberia long enough." Oh, so they've sent me to Siberia, have they! Well, thanks a lot. I have to say that I worked harder at Lasker as a chief, than I did at Wollman as a skate guard.

There have been several cases where members of the Wollman staff got mugged in the park as they walked from the rink to the subway on their way home from work. We had a night foreman, Mr. Bullroy, who nobody liked because he terrorized the night crew. He would go out on the ice after reconditioning and get down on his knees and feel the ice with his hand to make sure it was o.k. One night, he went a little too far and rubbed some of the Puerto Rican guys the wrong way. They all got mad and dumped sugar in his gas tank, cut the tires of his car and busted the windshield. They then pushed his car into the lake and threatened his life. He had to have a police escort out of the park that night.

One morning, as I was getting ready to spray the ice, there was a pile of snow that needed to be pushed off the ice before I could start spraying. I drove the tractor backwards down the ramp as this particular machine was too heavy at the front end to be driven forward, as the front wheels wouldn't go over the hump or edge of the ice. As I proceeded onto the ice backwards, I had my feet hanging down. I was wearing my skates and didn't want to ruin my blades or lose the edge off my blades by placing my feet on the metal running board of the tractor. The snow chains weren't tightly installed on the tires and as the wheels spun, one of the loose chains caught on the blade of one of my dangling skate. Let me tell you, I had found myself in what can only be accurately described as a predicament. Actually, I should have been snatched up off the seat and caught in the wheel. For a minute there, I really thought it was time for me to kiss the sun goodbye. However, as God and fate are always at my side, the chain for reasons beyond my comprehension, released my skate blade and my foot was now wedged between the wheel and the fender. My right foot was wedged under the fender and my body was on the opposite side of the tractor. The wheels were revolving slowly, as I had reduced the throttle to an idle. I was now hopping frantically on my left foot to keep up with the moving tractor in a very precarious position. I was desperately reaching across to the other side of the tractor.to reach the key switch that was located under the left side of the hood. Damn Fords! Why don't they buy Fergusons with the ignition on top! I did manage to shut the damn thing off. Where were the skate guards when you need them? Well, as usual, they are never around when you really need them. The old folks always said, "It's better to be born lucky than to be born rich," and I believe it, "God looks after children and fools." I don't reckon I have to wonder which category I fall into. When I got home that night, I think I got down on my knees and prayed a little harder than normal.

Lasker Rink closed in the middle of February and I was detailed back to Wollman. As the Borough Director had said, I had served my time in Siberia and would now be allowed to return to society. Well, what a society, it turned out to be. Although I was an ice chief, I had no established authority over the Wollman staff as they had their own chief and unless he was off or away, I was more or less ignored. Many of the guys who were there when I left had been replaced for whatever reason and the new guys who didn't know me, were downright resentful at my "coming down there and trying to tell them what to do."

Everyone was quite content to just lie around and sleep or smoke pot or shove needles into their arms to inject whatever concoction they could beg, borrow or steal. I told one of the guys to pour some gas into the jeep to which he replied, "No man, I'm not doing that and you can't make me do it." He became very indignant and wanted to call me out for a fist fight. He threatened to go home and get his gun and come back to shoot me. Well, I wasn't going to make him gas up the jeep. To get involved in a fight in order to make him work just wasn't part of my job.

If you go looking for a job, it's because you need one and if you need one, you can't be too independent after you get one. That is to say, on the job, you have to work willingly and readily and do whatever you're told to do. If you are told to shovel snow, you grab your shovel and start shoveling, if that's what you were hired to do. You can't tell your boss what you DON'T want to do or what you AIN'T going to do or nobody's going to MAKE you do. And, if you feel that way, then you shouldn't be working in the first place. As long as you are getting paid, you take orders and if you don't like what you're doing, quit and go someplace else. However, everyone doesn't see it that way. I just hope there will always be a Wollman Rink where these guys can work because they can't make it anywhere else.

Where is the supervisor? Oh, he's still in the office with his feet on the desk smoking his cigar and dreaming of being on the golf course. Oh well, at least I have the satisfaction of knowing that when Mr. Defazio was here, Wollman Rink was run like a well-oiled machine. Then on the other hand, with an attitude like mine, it doesn't always pay to work for somebody else. I can get out there and bust my rump 24 hours a day, 7 days a week, and 52 weeks out of the year. Maybe one day, I break a leg while working and can't do it anymore. Then they just cast me aside like an old worn out shoe and get somebody else. It is understood that the company or the department or the people you're working for don't care a damn for you, other than the amount of work you can do for them. Too bad it's like that, but that's the way it is. There are some supervisors and foremen, who are interested in building their reputations and have a hardnosed management style because they want their subordinates to know that they have power and they want to get the work done.

Well, being hard doesn't always necessarily get the job done. It can get your gas tank filled with sugar and I know a couple of bosses who would be the first to agree with me. I was told that the biggest goof-offs who worked in the Park Dept. always turned out to be the hardest bosses. You might do better by using diplomacy and psychology. I mean it doesn't hurt to pat a guy on the back every now and then and tell him what a good job he's doing, if he deserves it. Or recognize staff that has done good work, whether it's a permanent or seasonal worker. After all, we are all people trying to make a living.

It was nice to be back at Wollman, especially as I didn't have to work as hard as I did up at Lasker. But this new breed of skate guards they had at Wollman were totally unsatisfactory. Their uniforms never saw soap or water, were a light dark black and completely wrinkled. In less than three months they had gone from Wollman's finest to Wollman's wrinkliest.

If I had my way, I would cut away all the dead wood and start from scratch. It's a waste of time whipping a dead horse that includes the supervisor. After all, the crew is only as good as the leader. One day, I received a letter in the mail from the Arsenal which said that I should send in an envelope with a stamp on it and my address to receive back pay that I had coming. I did that and in about three days, I received the envelope back with a check for $400. Then I started thinking, that for two years, this can't even be half right. I sat down on the edge of the bed and calculated what I was owed. I concluded that I was owed close to $1200. Well, I didn't waste time getting over to the Arsenal to speak to the person responsible for these calculations. Meanwhile, my new bike which was now my old bike, felt like it was getting mighty small.

After I presented my case to the person responsible, she looked at me like I was crazy and didn't know what I was talking about. She pulled out my pay records and reviewed them and low and behold, confirmation. She informed me that I would receive the rest of my money in a couple of weeks. Ghost Motorcycles, here I come. When I went down to the rink and put the word out, it spread like wildfire throughout the Parks Dept. The seasonal workers descended on the Arsenal like a swarm of hungry locusts. The last I heard, that poor woman had barricaded herself in her office, leaving signs out like, "Out To Lunch," "On Vacation," "No Seasonals Allowed," "Write Me A Letter." To this very day, she can occasionally be detected moving stealthily around incognito.

The season came to an end and those of us who wanted to work were reassigned. My good friend, Bobby McDougal and I ended up at 79th Street Boat Basin. They had us picking up papers on Hudson River Drive. One day, we were told to go out into the park area around the boat basin and collect the dead chickens and goat-heads that were left behind by a group of local witches, hobgoblins and devil worshippers. These items were left in the park the previous weekend, by people involved in religious rites and rituals, and devil worship. Some of these carcasses had already started to decompose and the odor was horrific and turned our stomachs. Bobby said, "Why did Mary Boyle send me up here, with all this voodoo going on?" The following day, the foreman planned to send us someplace to mow grass. Then he got involved in a long drawn out discussion on the care of the lawn mower—how to pour in the gas and where to put the oil etc. We didn't want to appear to know more than he did, but after we thought this had gone far enough, we whipped out our park dept. licenses that indicated that we are qualified on every piece of equipment the park dept owned. He shut up after that.

At about that time, the phone rang and when he finished talking, he asked for two volunteers to be detailed over to the zoo to work with the mason. We volunteered, or should I say I volunteered and dragged Bobby along. Once we were at the zoo, we were introduced to Desediro. He was the mason and was waiting anxiously for our arrival. When we arrived, he assigned us unceremoniously, to the top of the rock pile, or should I say, mountain of stones.

Desediro was deeply involved in several renovation projects around the zoo. He completed a project in the birdhouse. He built a stone wall against an already existing wall, arranging the stones so that many of them projected outwards away from the wall, with vines hanging and water dripping. The wall created a tropical jungle effect. I must say, the birds enjoyed their new environment, they flew about singing merrily. He also built a panda cage in the Children's Zoo. There weren't any pandas in it yet. We were there to help Desediro build a wall in the llamas' cage, as well as build drinking fountains and water holes.

The first thing we had to do was carry stones into the cage where the wall was to be constructed. The stones varied in sizes from the size of a fist all the way up to the size of a cap stone on top of the Great Pyramid. To move these stones which had been dumped behind the zoo garage, we were given a wheel barrow and a hand truck. We had to dig under piles of mud and dirt to reach the stones that were brought in whenever a load was requested from construction sites elsewhere. The stones weren't very clean. Poor Bobby cried all day as he complained, "Man! You know what I'm gonna do to you . . . What the hell you got us into now?" "Aw, you ain't gonna do nothing lemon, so just quit belly-aching and pick up the stones."

The mason, who was a hard worker and very nice person, had requested a front end loader to move the larger stones. After completing the job in the bird house, he said that he was invited to the Arsenal and he showed us a photograph of himself and the dignitaries there. "That's me there, said the mason, pointing to a figure, standing in back of the crowd of high officials and politicians from the Arsenal. The tail end of the donkey, I break my ass doing all the work and they knock each other down to be the first to take credit for my work". With a noticeable amount of bitterness in his voice he continued, "I spent a whole day getting my suit pressed, nails manicured, shaved and showered because I had been invited to the Arsenal to celebrate. I should've stayed home. I get up there and what do I get—half of a doughnut and half a cup of coffee. These guys are all supposed to be millionaires. When they took the picture, they almost left me out of it, and I'm supposed to be the guest of honor!"

NYC Mayor Michael Bloomberg, Marvin Brown and Commissioner
Adrian Benipee

CHAPTER VIII

He then motioned toward 5th Avenue with a trowel he was holding in his hand. They will use all their influence and money to make sure that these s.o.bs stay in office so that they can all continue to make all the money, meanwhile poor bastards like you and me have to get out here every day and break our ass for nothing. Well, I had no real knowledge of the workings of politics and politicians, but I agreed with him anyway. By the end of the day I was so tired, I could hardly get home. I hadn't done that much work since leaving Lasker.

The following day we had help, such as it was, of a roving gang. That's a crew of men assigned to ride around in a truck and do whatever odd jobs that might come up in any given park. They would load their hand truck up with the smallest stones and not too many of them, and then, the entire crew, pushing one hand truck and getting all in the way of each other would spend half an hour figuring out and discussing the best way to get the hand truck over the hump and to where the stones were needed. Needless to say, the mason, who was a let's-do-it-and-get-over with type of fellow, said to me, "Watch this guy," pointing to one short guy with a cigar in his mouth who was fiddling with his gloves. "We call him frozen brains. He puts his gloves on and takes them off 75 times a minute. This way he never has to do any work. Oh, he's smarter than you think he is. When there's something to do, he has to put on his gloves first and by the time he gets his gloves on, the work is all done. So, then he takes his gloves off again. No, he's not at all dumb." After I had observed the frozen brains guy, he pointed to the truck.

"You see that guy sitting in the truck, he's our MVO. He's so fat he can't even get out of the truck. He has trouble turning the steering wheel because his stomach gets in the way." After a half a day of grumbling and complaining about what they were doing and threatening to put in a grievance to the union rep, the roving gang was ordered someplace else. They probably left with hopes of finding a better place to hide, as there were too many high ranking park officials walking through this area. Only Rocky stayed behind and while he and I were carrying the stones, Bobby was mixing the cement and serving it to the mason. While I was busy on the rock pile, a black car pulled into the zoo parking lot. Someone stepped out and slammed the door and a familiar voice said, "Hello Marvin, how are you doing?"

I looked up from what I was doing and greeted my old friend and former boss Mr. Joe Dee. He then said, "It looks hard Marvin, it sure looks hard! I assured him that indeed it was, after which he continued off to the Arsenal about whatever business he had there. Meanwhile, I had a short conversation with his chauffeur who was an MVO friend of mine from Lasker Rink. His name was Gilbert. Gilbert told me that Mr. Joe Dee was on his way into the Arsenal to be officially made Borough Director of Staten Island, a job he had been seeking for a long time. He lives out there and it's convenient for him to get to work. My guess is that he's just lying low there until he sees a good chance to spring board into City Hall as Mayor. Well, I hope he runs as a democrat because I'll never vote for another republican for anything, no matter who he is.

I received a letter from Greg. The army sent him to Berlin, Germany where he had been assigned to a most unexpected job as a life guard in the officer's swimming pool. He included a photograph of the pool. He also said that his mother had sent him his skates and he went skating everyday at a place called Olympic Stadium and they didn't use skate guards. He said that skating there wasn't as organized the way it was at Wollman. People skated whatever way they wanted to, clockwise, counter clockwise, across traffic, all at the same time. He said, he met a nice girl whose name was Connie and that he was going to marry her at the end of his tour of duty.

I wrote back to him that I wished him well and lots of luck and that I was glad he didn't have to go to Vietnam. Bobby and his wife Elaine were scheduled to go to Europe for three weeks and planned to visit Holland, Denmark, Finland, Germany and everything in between. While they were away, I was supposed to keep his car and look after their dog and apartment. And by the time he returned to New York, it would be time to start work at the pool, so he resigned from the Rock Pile and he and Elaine were off to Europe. A week, later a postcard came to the zoo addressed to the mason. It had a picture of a nude Dutch girl, standing behind a sign which read "Here is something to make your job more interesting." It was signed Bobby. Meanwhile, I wasn't having an easy time looking after his car. Every time I drove it, it fell apart. One day the muffler fell off, another day the door handle fell off, another time a window fell out. Meanwhile, I had to spend my money for these repairs because he would say it was my fault.

One night while it was storming, my brother James, who was in the Navy asked me to drive him out to Staten Island where his ship was in dry dock. It was around 11 o'clock at night and raining cats and dogs as I was driving over the bridge to Staten Island. Just as I reached the top, the accelerator pedal fell from under my foot and dropped down through the floor. After stopping on top of the bridge, then getting down on the ground and crawling around under the VW bus on my back, in the rain and filth and catching double pneumonia and triple TB, I finally located the trouble as being a broken accelerator cable that ran from the pedal back to the rear where the engine is located. Damn you Bobby! My brother took a bus to his ship after a bridge authority truck had pushed us off the bridge. I left the car parked on the side of the road and went home on the bus and subway. I took a hot bath and went to bed and had nightmares about Bobby's car being stripped or stolen. I really expected to find it sitting on milk crates. After running all over town to every VW dealer, who either didn't have the cable I wanted or wouldn't sell it to me, I finally managed to get my hands on one at a place on Staten Island. When I returned to pick up the car, to my surprise, it was still there and intact. I then installed the cable. Bobby probably left the car with me so I could fix the damn thing. Afterwards I drove back to West 78th Street to look after his stupid dog, a big Afghan hound that he and Elaine paid $400 for. The dog could eat more pork sausages and wheatina than I could. I took the dog up the street and behind the Museum of Natural History to let her run loose, as I was told to do. When I got ready to go, it was all I could do to catch that long-legged fool. I sure wished they would hurry up and come back here, so they could look after their own problems.

The wall progressed slowly on until it was finished. We decorated the water holes in each cage with small stones and Desidero even carved, or maybe I should say scratched, our names into the cement of one of the fountains along with the date. Bobby and Elaine returned from their trip and we went to the Arsenal for reappointment to our pools. Bobby related all the interesting things that he had done while in Europe. He said they'd had a nice time in Holland, Germany and Denmark but instead of going to Finland, Elaine wanted to go to Paris and Rome so they took the train down to France. When they got to Paris, it was so much more expensive than all the other places they had been. Instead of going to Rome, they decided it would be best to head home.

When they first got to Paris, they weren't too familiar with French style bathroom fixtures. When they had to urinate, they used what they thought was the toilet. When it wouldn't flush away, Bobby went to find the chamber maid who promptly informed him that, "Monsieur, zat ezz not zee toilet. Zat ezz zee foot bath."

With all this back pay burning a hole in my pocket, I took a ride out to Ghost Motorcycles to see if they had something that came a little closer to measuring up to my now higher developed skills as a motorcyclist. Once I arrived there, a salesman took me to three warehouses to look at bikes. They had bikes stacked from the floor to the ceiling. I didn't know there were that many bikes in existence. The owner, Sal started out by selling two bikes that a New Jersey importer sold him. When the importer returned, he bought two more bikes to sell, and now 20 years later, he was the largest dealer on the east coast.

I settled on a red and silver BSA Lightening which was selling for $1300. My own bike and the money from the Parks Dept., was enough to cover the cost and insurance. Sitting proudly on my new road burner, I rode into the city and as I was riding through the Greenwich Village, I decided I'd swing across 8th Street and stop over at Ham Fish Pool to see Bobby. As I stopped for a light on the corner of Second Avenue, I was suddenly surrounded by four cops who demanded my license, and registration. They asked "Where did you get this motorcycle?"

"Hey, this is a new motorcycle! Where is the serial number on the frame? Where is the serial number on the engine? Is this a motorcycle license?" They were harassing me. I didn't dislike cops, as such, but it was obvious that as long as I rode a motorcycle, I wasn't going to have many friends in blue. After ten minutes of being hassled around, I guess they were satisfied that I owned the motorcycle and allowed me to go my way. On the other hand, there are a lot of stolen bikes around this area. I guess they really are doing a good thing after all. Anyway, since that time, I avoid Greenwich Village like the plague.

Once I arrived at Ham Fish, I pulled up outside the filter house and blew my horn. The door opened and Bobby told me to come in. There were a few people hanging around outside admiring my bike. I didn't plan to be inside long enough for anybody to put it in his pocket and disappear. Anyway, I left the door open. As I got inside the door, a large cap stone fell from the roof and landed on the ground where, only two seconds before, I had been standing. Well, I knew I had made some enemies here and there, but I didn't know I had any in this area.

Bobby said, "Man, you can't leave your bike out there!" So I turned around and thought to bring my bike inside, but when I got outside the door, somebody had disconnected the spark plug leads and somebody else was busy screwing out the spark plugs and they were still hot. When I came out they ran off, so I fixed everything back the way it was. Bobby told me once, that if anybody wanted to buy parts for their car in that area, they only needed to go into any auto store and ask for what they wanted. If they didn't have it in stock, they would send someone out into a parking lot or wherever there were parked cars with desired parts, and just strip it off. They would have the part in less than a half hour. Bearing all this in mind, I thought that I should leave before those street urchins started to take me apart and jumped on my new horse and blazed a trail of burnt rubber, sand and rocks, and burned my way across Houston Street to FDR Drive.

Several years later, a filter plant operator lost his life in that very same place. Murdered and robbed by some of those, know nothing, do nothing, be nothing, non productive bad elements, hanging around outside the filter house door. I don't know what the circumstances were surrounding the case, but from what I read in the papers, I would say that, a sixteen year old kid, new to the job opened the door and some thugs came in and killed him. It was unfortunate that this young kid didn't understand that you just don't open the door to the filter plant. All kinds of curiosity seekers come to the filter house during the day and at night, wanting to know who you are, what you do and how does this thing or that thing work. And they'll tell you in a quick minute that they ain't leaving and you can't make them leave. This kid didn't know that because there was no one of experience there to tell him. The two guys that were there before him, namely Che'o and Lawrence, were big, mean and tough and the killers would have thought twice of entering the plant to do mischief. In fact, the new kid was there to replace one of them. I don't know which one. I routinely stayed inside the filter house with the door closed and locked. I normally worked midnight to eight, the same shift this kid worked when he died. I not only locked the door, I barred it shut with pipes and planks just for good measure. What happens if there is a chlorine leak? Well, I'll take my chances with the chlorine, because I know what to expect if we have a leak. I honestly believe that if this poor kid would have been better trained on securing the plant, he would be alive today. I have heard people outside of the door of my filter house discussing the best way to pick off the night watchman, with a gun they had.

The night watchman, who normally sits outside the office on the pool deck, is the guy that was supposed to chase these same people out of the pool. One night watchman was afraid of his own shadow. I remember a time when Tom tried to chase somebody out of the pool and instead of leaving the pool, they went over to the office with a bottle which they broke and tried to cut him with the broken glass. He came running over to my side of the pool yelling for help. When I went over, they had gone, but I still had to baby sit him the rest of the night. Yes, he called the police, they arrived three hours later. It was good to be working at Sunset again or so I thought. I hadn't yet met the supervisor, who had been off the first week that I was there. When he did come in, my first thought was, "Oh sweat, a hippie supervisor!"

He ordered the regular men to bring out the pool paint, rollers and brushes, and paint the pool. I didn't marvel very long over this guy looking like a hippie. He came to the filter house and told me to put on my hip boots and go out and help paint the pool. I was shocked and surprised at his request because painting the pool wasn't part of my job. To my knowledge, no filter plant operator has ever been ordered to paint the pool before. It was a job for laborers who are paid 12 thousand dollars a year more than SPM's. In any case, I decided that I couldn't afford to quit just now and he had me over a barrel. So, I put on my boots and went out and took up my position. All of the regular men were painting the wall in one direction, so I decided to paint in the opposite direction. Since I had to do this, I decided I just as soon do it and get it over with. After I completed painting the longest wall, I passed the corner and headed into the home stretch. Then I heard the supervisor say to one regular man who spent a good deal of his time in one spot, "Come on Joe, let's go! Look at Brown over there he's just about painted the entire pool by himself." Would you believe, that Joe came over to me and said, "What the hell you doing Brown? Trying to show me up? You take it easy! You're making me look bad in front of the boss."

He was overlooking the fact that I was actually helping him, because my job was inside the filter house, not outside painting the pool. Well, that was Friday. The next day I came in, two laborers were painting the pool. They informed me that the boss left word for me to help them paint the pool. I decided that I would quit. While I don't mind working, painting the pool isn't what I was hired to do, so I told them to tell the boss that I quit. I went over to Bobby's pool to see what he was doing. He too, was painting but inside the filter house, not outside in the pool. After he finished painting, we went across to the office to call his wife. His foreman was there sitting at the desk. Willie Ha-Ha, a Dept. of Parks worker was also there. He was called Willie Ha-Ha, because he had some kind of nervous laugh and between every two words he would say ha, ha. Anyway, the foreman told Willie Ha-Ha to go to the park and clean up the playground. There was another guy standing there with a can of paint. He sent him to paint the ceiling of the first aid room which is located at one end of the filter house.

I think the foreman just wanted to get rid of them for a while because as soon as they left, he went to the filing cabinet, opened it and pulled out a dead soldier (empty bottle of whiskey). He gave it a long, hard disbelieving look and tossed it into the garbage can. He dug a little deeper into his filing cabinet and pulled out a live one, broke the seal and leaned back, put the bottle to his mouth and took three or four good swallows before he put it back in the file cabinet. About this time, Willie Ha-Ha came back dragging behind him half of a dead tree in one hand and an old rusty bed spring in the other. He dragged these things right into the office and said, "I found this out in the park!" The foreman was really at a loss for words. He said, "What the hell . . . where are you going with that stuff?" He then jumped up and out of his chair and pointed toward the front door and said, "Get that stuff out of here." Willie Ha-Ha obeyed. The foreman said to me, "Can you really believe this?" If they find old chairs, animals or dead bodies in the park, they drag it in here and drop it at my feet."

He then turned around to his filing cabinet for his bottle and took another swig. This time, there was someone banging on the door which opened into the pool side. The guy who was supposed to be painting the ceiling was begging to be let in because it was raining. When the foreman saw who it was, he said, "Leave him out there!" He then got up and opened the door himself and said, "What do you want now?" When the guy came in he said, "I climbed up on the ladder and the paint fell off and spilled over the floor. Can you give me two guys to help me clean it up?"

The foreman exploded, "Are you out of your mind? First, you want me to send someone to help you paint this small ceiling which shouldn't take more than an hour for one man, and now, you want me to send somebody over there to clean up what you messed up! I don't believe you people! Get out of here, get back over there and clean it up!" The guy made his exit and the foreman who now had both hands over his head, turned once more to his filing cabinet, as he said, "I'm going out of my mind." He took, two swallows and said, "I don't think I'm going to last much longer, these people are driving me crazy!" Bobby and I died laughing. It was much more pathetic than it was funny. I can't help but wonder how the city managed to systematically accumulate so many zeros in one place. But even zeros have to earn a living. I wonder if the other city departments function the same way. I get the impression that anybody with a small amount of ambition could join a city dept and start from the bottom and work his way all the way up to the Mayor's job, if he wanted to. I'll bet if private corporations were run the way some city depts. are, they would be bankrupt and out of business in a very short time.

How do you make people work? Especially employees that are employed by the city! If a guy is hired to work a job, and on his first day on the job, he sees that he's held accountable and hard work and results are valued, he'll work hard and do his best. However, if a guy is hired to work and on the first day on the job, his fellow workers feel that he is doing too much, and tell him to slow down and take it easy, and no one is held accountable for their work, so he slows down, and maybe everybody has the attitude that they're not going to do anymore than they have to, since they're going to get paid anyway.

Whether they work fast or slow, or not at all, they are still going to get the same pay, and indeed they're still going to get paid. In a case like that, the best thing to do is dump the whole lot and start new. However, you can't do that in a city department, or at least not in New York City, as there is a law against firing city employees. So, the most a city supervisor can do, is bring a guy up on charges, and maybe fine him a couple of days pay. After that, he'll probably put in for a transfer, and in his new place of work, go back to his old routine. Then too, you can have ten good men working and you hire one more, and this one doesn't want to work, and he's not going to work or let anybody else work. He starts grumbling and bullying all the other guys, and pretty soon he drags the entire crew down with him, and now you've got eleven men who are not going to work. This is the case of a one bad apple in the barrel that spoils the entire barrel.

In this case maybe you can shake a little life into them or out of them by setting a few examples starting with the trouble maker. By getting rid of him and maybe a couple of others, you might be able to salvage the rest. Of course a man usually puts in a good days work, if indeed he'll work at all, when there's some kind of end reward. It doesn't matter if the reward is a lot of money or just a permanent position with benefits with the city, instead of a permanent seasonal position with no benefits.

The Laborer's test can only be taken by someone who's already in the department or someone who's already an attendant. And every time the attendant's test is given, I was out of the country. I once took a test for a position with the transit authority, passed with a score of 85 and was number 2,000 on the list. I was called four years later to take the physical exam, which I failed, because of my heart murmur. I didn't think having a heart murmur was very serious since I was working a physically strenuous job as a skate guard. I also erroneously thought that because I failed the physical exam, I wouldn't be qualified to work in the Parks Dept. However, this is all a diversion from the real story.

Around 9 o'clock on Monday my phone rang. I answered and it was Frank Pollino, who was the number one man at the pool, or assistant to the bosses. He said, in his slow talking Brooklyn accent, "Listen Brown, I heard what happen and I told the boss you're not supposed to be painting the pool. I can't blame you for wanting to quit. Why don't you go back to the filter plant. You can't quit on us now. You're a good man." I went back over there and busied myself in the filter house, later one of the regular men came over and told me, "You know Brown, if you want to get along with this guy, meaning the general foreman "you gotta keep a bottle in your locker and whenever he comes over here, pour him up a good stiff drink and he'll leave you alone." Well that's exactly what I did. The thing is, he only left me alone until the next time he got thirsty and I must say we became friends after that. He later said, "Brown, I'm sorry I made you paint the pool, but the office doesn't send me as much help as I need. On Thursday, I filled up the swimming pool and since the pumps wouldn't start I had to back it in. This is done by closing the influent valves at the filters and opening the main return drain from the pool. This allows the water from the city water supply valve, which opens into the treatment tank, to go directly into the pool through the return drain

City of New York
Parks & Recreation

This is to certify that

Marvin Brown

SPMO, 5 Boro Technical Services

is Operations'

Employee of the Month

for September 2003

Liam Kavanagh
First Deputy Commissioner

Adrian Benepe
Commissioner

Employee of the Month Certificate

Light of the World Award

CHAPTER IX

Friday morning the electricians came over to repair the pumps, and I was able to allow the water to circulate and fill the diving pool. Then, every kid hanging around outside the fence began climbing over the fence and jumping into the pool, always the deep pool. Some time ago, a kid jumped off the high board into two feet of water and cracked his head. There was even a life guard who jumped off the high board into the scum gutter and cracked his head.

Later in the day, as the water level in the deep part of the pool came closer to the top, a little kid ran over to tell me that there was a kid who jumped in and never came up. I didn't really believe him, as kids bother me all day with such talk. I didn't think that someone who couldn't swim would jump into 16 feet of water. I decided to go over and take a look. The water was so muddy you couldn't see the bottom. Well, by the time I got over to the edge of the pool, somebody was bringing the boy up the ladder and I helped to get him up onto the deck. Although his eyes were open or staring, he didn't show any other signs of life. While someone was administering artificial respiration, I ran over to the office and called the police. They came with an ambulance and took the kid to the Lutheran Hospital. I later learned that the doctors had managed to get his heart beating but couldn't get him to breathe or maybe it was the other way around. In any case, he died and was only 12 years old.

The ranking officials blamed the supervisor who had gone to the office to pick up our paychecks. I can't see where it was his fault, as the city was trying to save money and didn't assign two life guards to work when the pool was filled. The supervisor was promptly transferred over to Red Hook or as he put it, "They threw me into the briar patch." They sent us a new supervisor who walked enthusiastically around looking over the place like he was trying to make up his mind whether he should buy it or not. He would follow me around the filter plant, asking a lot of questions about how it functioned and sometimes even getting in my way, but that's beside the point. The boss isn't always right, but the boss is always the boss. Anyway, he was a good man.

On Monday, my number 2 man, Pete Suchanick came in and on Wednesday the number 3 man came. He said he had been a skate guard chief at the Abe Stark Rink in Coney Island and his name was Tony. That alone was bad news to me. At least all the lemons they send me have the same name, Tony. This way I can spot them right away. Which reminds me of a MVO from the Manhattan garage whose name was Tony. This Tony developed a reputation for being what the department calls a stiff. He turned over a packer loader, which is another way of saying garbage truck, and had driven over a fire hydrant with one of the front end loaders and had various other infractions on his record. So, in order to get rid of him, dispatchers sent him over to Lasker Rink.

Anyway, getting back to Tony, I'd spent two days explaining to him how the plant worked and generally showing him what his job was, but he just didn't seem to understand anything I said. In fact, he appeared to be in some kind of daze. I would point out a valve, and explain what it was used for and five minutes later I would ask him a question on it. He wouldn't even remember me ever talking about it. He only had two days to pick it up before opening day. At which time he would be on his own. I soon realized that he was high on some kind of dope. He also started selling dope from the filter house to people out in the park and they would come around day and night looking for Tony. "Are you Tony? Well, when is he going to be here, I'll be back then. Tell him someone wants to see him. He'll know why." At that time, I couldn't understand why the hell everyone was so interested in him. But that was before I realized what was going on.

The summer was off to a dramatic start because the next thing that happened was the wall of the pool split open, dumping all the water into the tunnel and back onto the floor of the filter plant. This happened sometime during Tony's shift. He went home or some place, and was so high that he didn't know anything about it anyway. He didn't even care. I called him at home, realizing it was me, he hung up the phone. It wasn't his fault that the wall split and he just didn't care. I sure don't know how he ever got hired. I guess, at those indoor rinks you don't have to know much. Or maybe it's who you know. The Fire Dept came and pumped out the filter plant over night and the shops sent out the required mechanics to do the necessary repairs. The plant was started to circulate the water that was left in the pool, and that wasn't much. It was soon discovered that the pool wouldn't hold water anymore. It was discovered that both of the longer walls of the pool were split. There were already many cracks in the wall. They just got bigger. On one wall, the cracks were above the underwater lights. The other, the crack was below the lights. I took a walk around inside the tunnel and I noticed that the cracks were almost half the length of that of the wall and there was another crack in the center of one shorter end wall. Whenever I added water to the pool, it only ran right out again. The water ran onto the floor of the filter plant.

If these cracks aren't fixed, when the summer session begins and the pool is filled up again, the dampness will expand the walls once again. Maybe, the wall developed a crack in it during the contraction process last winter. When the pool is full of water again and the wall expands, the crack which is part of the wall is also going to close.

This was a job for the mason from Brooklyn Shops, so someone named McGreevie, who I figured must've been somebody big in the Borough Office, came around to take a look to determine what exactly should be done. The following morning around 10 o'clock, a big truck pulled up outside the gate. I unlocked the gate and let them in. They were the masons. After taking 45 minutes to get ready to work, they went down into the tunnel and did a bit of chipping and chopping until 11:45. They came up and said they were going to lunch. They ate lunch, then they just lay around on the pool deck and sunned themselves on the bleachers. They borrowed my beach chair and just really got into acting like they were down in Miami lounging around the Fontainebleau. At about 1:30, they all got up, stretched, yawned and lazily found their way back down into the tunnel. They didn't even replace my beach chair. Promptly at 2:30, they started to prepare to leave. They must get ready to go back to Prospect Park to make sure they're there in time to sign out and go home.

I think I'll get a job like that. Any half wit knows that if you have to work, your whole life through, then the city is the way to go.

After about two weeks, I was able to bring the pool level almost to the top without losing too much water back into the filter plant. Of course, these masons worked that way all summer and every summer after that. I just started dumping aluminum sulfate directly into the pool, and the pool leaks slowed down noticeably or until I no longer had to wade through water on the floor of the filter plant. The aluminum sulfate becomes sticky and gummy once it gets wet, and was carried into the cracks by the water draining through the cracks. It then formed a gummy seal and slowed the flow of water.

Of course, the proper thing to do is to bring in an outside contractor sometime during the winter or early spring and let him open up the cracks from inside the pool and seal it up once and for all. I was tired of having to go through the same leaky hassle every year. We had another drowning during the middle of the season. A 20-year old, who was high on dope, so I heard, climbed over the fence around 11:30 p.m. and jumped in the pool. He swam out to the middle of the deep pool and went down and didn't come up again. Someone knocked on the filter house door and said, "Put the lights on because there was someone at the bottom of the pool." I turned the lights on and came out to check the pool. By the time I got to the pool, the person had been down there for around 20 minutes and it was now 10 minutes before midnight. There was supposed to be a cop stationed there until midnight, but someone outside the gate side said that he left about a quarter past 11. The night watchman called the police who, at around midnight, came running, all ten of them. None of them wanted to get into the water to bring up the body, and the person who did get into the water was one of the people from out in the park. He happened to be a good friend of the victim and was so grief stricken that he had to make about 5 attempts before he succeeded in towing the body over the edge of the pool, so that someone could get a hand on it. In other words, he would go down to the bottom and bring the body up to the top, then he would be overcome with grief and let go again, and then go back down for another try. Everybody just stood around looking. I can't swim myself and even though I've worked many years in the filter plant, I was careful and didn't take any unnecessary chances.

Even though I feel that I understand death and dying, and maybe even what happens afterwards, the whole thing in itself might not be as bad as it seems to most people. I still think that suffocating in the water is a bad way to go. The private companies that manufacture and install private pools also manufacture and install pool covers. Some of these covers can be moved into position at the press of a button. It really wouldn't be such a bad idea to investigate the use of pool covers for city pools, or at least covers for the deep pools. To me, the worse drowning to date, was the little kid who was pulled from Sunset Pool at 8 a.m. on opening day during the 1973 season. He had been missing from home since the evening of the day before.

One of our SPMs walked over to the deep pool to clean the deck and went to the office to tell us that there was a body in the pool. One of the life guards brought him up, only 8 years old. It really breaks me up when these young kids die that way, especially since they didn't even get to live yet. I believe that the parents are to blame, because when their kids are young, they should know where they are at night or even better, keep them home. The pool closed on Labor Day and we had a couple of weeks left before we would start at the rink. Bobby and I were invited by some Finnish friends of ours, the Mataanens, to come out to Long Island the following weekend. They had a country house there with a sauna in the basement.

Well, we went out there and got undressed and went into the sauna. Zackie started throwing water on the hot rocks. We really started to perspire or should I say, we were being cooked. After about two minutes, Bobby jumped up, screamed and almost broke down the door getting out. I stayed in for two minutes more and then I did the same thing, with the exception of the scream. We all put our towels around us and went out back and jumped into the ocean to cool off. After we cooled off, we returned to the sauna for another frying treatment. Zackie is a UN reporter for a Finnish newspaper and his wife Pia is one of Eileen Ford's star models. They told us a story about the Finnish troops during the war. They had captured some Russians soldiers and for sanitary reasons forced them into a hot sauna. One of the Russian soldiers burst out and begged, "Please don't fry me, shoot me instead!"

We spent much of the day in and out of the sauna and nude in the ocean. All the neighbors were on their roofs with telescopes. Afterwards, we were supposed to use a special type of brush to make our skin tough. But as they couldn't find them in New York, they didn't have any. I know that from the point of view of most

Americans, the whole affair is supposed to be something very erotic. However, I didn't find anything erotic in it at all. Indeed, all this eroticism is only in the mind of the beholder. We later ate a very delicious Finnish dinner.

When we got back into the Mahattan, someone told us that a skate guard had committed suicide. He was one of the Wollman guys and his name was Rubin Fernandez. He was on dope with a very big habit and his wife was trying to make him stop. At some point, she decided that it couldn't be done and she left him. When he realized that he couldn't live without her, he decided to take his life. So, he went down into the subway tunnel and climbed down on the tracks. After standing behind one of the supports to wait for a suitable train to come along, he threw himself into the path of an express train. Sad but true.

I went back to Lasker Rink for the winter and all the problems I left there were still there. Mr. Bookbinder told me that the place didn't even function properly as a swimming pool. During the summer, they would fill the pool it up with water and it would lose half of it overnight. There's no need of going into all of the same problems, as I would only be repeating myself. However, there was one nice thing that happened. It was on November 15th, which was my birthday. We were out doing the ice, and right in the middle of reconditioning, one guy whose name was Freddie, went inside and took off his skates and came out and said he was going out to the store. We hadn't even finished with the ice yet. Well needless to say, I wasn't going to have that and I was ready to sign him out for the rest of the day. The boss came out and told me to let him go because he had something important to do.

Just as we were finishing the ice, he came back carrying a large box. All the guys put away their shovels and rushed into the locker room ahead of me. When I got inside the locker room, the boss and all the guys and all the personnel were waiting. They all shouted, "Surprise," and then they started singing, "For he's a jolly good fellow, for he's a jolly good fellow, which nobody can deny." On the table was a large white cake trimmed in red and on top of the cake was a little toy jeep pulling a toy cutter and box, and toy skate guards. Happy Birthday Chief," was written across the cake with a single candle burning on top. I was very surprised. As far as I can remember, I believe it was the first birthday cake I had ever gotten. I didn't remember ever telling anyone that it was my birthday. In any case, I didn't expect my birthday would mean anything to anybody other than me.

Being raised by my grandfather on the farm, birthdays were hardly an occasion to rejoice. My old man would say that buying birthday presents and such other foolishness would be an extravagance and an unnecessary waste of money. He figured if you had a shirt on your back and food in your stomach, you didn't need anything else. Of course, we had our own farm and equipment and a house and plenty to eat, and so did most folks in and around where we lived. I really think that I've benefitted greatly from his philosophy. In any case, they could see how surprised and speechless I was about this thoughtful gesture. The boss said, "Many Happy Returns" and that my getting fired from Wollman was the best thing that ever happened to him. I expressed my appreciation for everything and someone gave me a knife to cut the cake. I passed out slices to all until there was none left. Someone brought in a case of cokes and we really had a good time. It was very nice. And to think, I wanted to sign out the guy who bought the cake. I really hated myself.

A Swedish girlfriend of a friend of mine invited me to go to Sweden to. She said that in the city where she lived, Gothenburg, there were plenty of jobs and she would be glad to help me find a job and a place to stay. So I figured, why not. New York already had lost its glamour for me and besides, I was really getting too big to be a skate guard. So, at the end of the next pool season, I sold my bike, packed up my measly belongings and bade the "Naked City" farewell. Before I left the house, a telegram arrived for me. It read, "Pick up letter at the information desk at the Copenhagen Airport. My brother along with a couple of friends took me to the airport. I had already bought my ticket at the Scandinavian Airlines ticket office in the Manhattan earlier in the week. They announced my flight and I walked as far as the door of the ramp to board the plane. I turned around to say goodbye to the people with me and the tears welled up in my eyes and I almost changed my mind and maybe I should have. I felt like I was going off some place far away from my relatives, friends, familiar surroundings and probably might not ever come back. As indeed I was, though nobody was forcing me. My brother who worked for TWA picked my seat on the plane. There were a few babies on board and they steadily cried the entire 4 or 5 thousand miles to Copenhagen.

Once in Copenhagen, I stopped at the information desk and picked up the letter. When I opened it inside was the money I had given her to arrange a place for me to stay and the letter said in part, "Don't come to Gothenburg, go to Stockholm, there's no job, no place to stay and I can't help you." Don't come! Hell, I'm already here. My heart started to beat a little faster and the rest of me burst out in a sweat. Well, I couldn't go to Stockholm now because I had another suitcase coming through airfreight and it wouldn't be along for another couple of days and besides that, it was addressed to Gothenburg. My body was really going though some chemistry changes and I really wasn't feeling too well. With the envelope, letter and money still in my hand, I went to look for my connecting flight to Gothenburg. When I got on the plane and sat down, I shoved everything I had in my hand, including the money, down into my coat pocket, or so I thought I did. However, when I reached for the money later at the Gothenburg Airport, it wasn't in my pocket. I was probably so mad that I shoved it down between the seats. It was only $30, but I sure could have used it.

My passport was stamped in Copenhagen so I didn't have to have it stamped again in Sweden. Once you're inside Demark, Norway, Sweden and Finland, you can go from one to the other without having to show your passport at the borders. However, you would probably need to show it at the hotel for identification purposes, so you better keep it with you all the time. I stepped up to the airport bank window and changed some money. I had around $450, but I wasn't planning to spend it all in one place. I was planning to spend as little as possible and then only when absolutely necessary. So, I got into a taxi and told him to take me to the cheapest hotel in town. After riding all over the place and being told by various hotels that they had no rooms or that all their rooms were reserved, I managed to find one in a hotel across the plaza from the train station. Although I don't smoke, I bought three cartons of cigarettes at the airport in New York with the intention of giving them to the girl in Gothenburg. I gave the cab driver one for a tip, he almost fell over on the floor. I later learned why, cigarettes in Sweden cost over $5 a pack.

The room was three dollars a day, very clean and quite comfortable. The bed was somewhat smaller than what we call a twin bed and had a stack of mattresses on it. When I lay down on top of them, I sank right in. They folded over double with me inside, giving me the feeling of being swallowed up. It was quite comfortable too.

Later, I went out just as there was a fire in the next block. As I walked past, on the opposite side of the street, a crowd had gathered to watch the fireman work and I stopped to watch too. But everybody stopped watching the fire and turned around to look at me, so I rushed on down the street as if on some urgent business. As an African American, I was very conspicuous. I found a phone booth and called up the girl who invited me to Sweden. She almost fell on the floor when she realized it was me.

"I told you not to come here, didn't you get my letter?" I assured her that I did get her letter and that as soon as my luggage comes, I was going to Stockholm. She then told me, I should go to the local park and talk to some of the local hippies sitting around the fountain. Maybe, some of them would take me home with them and I wouldn't need to stay in a hotel. I wasn't about to do any such thing. I walked around window shopping and generally checking the place out. I almost got run over by one of those big oversize iron buses (trolley cars) that was running down the railroad track in the middle of the street. I was feeling ever so lonely. Here I was, in a strange country, where people were speaking a strange language that I didn't understand, and I had no place to go.

I was half way around the world with no friends or anyone I could call on. I later learned that my friend brought with her from New York another guy who was a draft dodger and who she had promised to introduce to the good life. Once they arrived in Copenhagen, she hit him with the bad news and left him stranded. On Tuesday afternoon, my bag arrived at the airport and I picked it up and checked out of the hotel. I bought a one way ticket to Stockholm and boarded the train. It left at 4 p.m. and was due at Stockholm's Central Station at 10 p.m. This was the first time that I rode a train that got to where it was supposed be at the time it was supposed to get there. When I arrived at the train station in Stockholm, I went to the Tourist Information window and inquired about a place to stay. They gave me the address of the KFUM (YMCA) and told me to take the subway, where to get off and which way to go after I got off. Well, I got on the subway and rode too far. I passed my stop, and then passed the last stop without realizing it. When the subway reached the place where the motorman has to change ends, I was the only one on the train. That should have told me something.

When the motorman was changing ends, he had to walk back along a sort of cat walk, along the outside of the train and as he was passing the car where I was sitting, he stopped and peered through the window. He probably wondered, why is that fool doing sitting in there. I managed to get back to the station where I was supposed to get off in the first place. When I left the station, I asked some people where the KFUM was located. They told me to go down this hill and make a right and go one hundred meters and make a left. However, having no concept of how much a meter was, or even how far one meter was, I walked too far and had to stop a passing police car and ask them. They told me to walk back 200 meters and there I would see a small road to my right. Well, I decided I'd concentrate on finding the road, instead of counting meters. After all, I knew what a road was. I found the road after stumbling around in the dark a while. I managed to find the place which was located behind a group of oil storage tanks along the docks. It's a wonder I didn't fall in the water.

The man signed me up and accepted 15 crowns ($3.00). He took me up to a room where there were six bunk beds and five of them were occupied. Now, the last place I wanted to sleep was in a strange country, in a strange room, where five strange men were sleeping, in five strange beds. I was supposed to sleep in the 6th bed. I hoped that everybody was asleep. I got undressed and rolled up my pants with my $400 still in them. I climbed up into the bed and put my pants under the pillow with my arms wrapped tightly around it. I slept with one eye open.

Bright and early the next morning, before the sun or anybody else was up, I got dressed. Making sure my $400 was still intact, I got to stepping. My pants were wrinkled, but that didn't bother me as long as they had the $400 still in them. On my way out, the man at the desk wanted to know if I was coming back that night and I replied, "Not if I find a room." He sounded very satisfied as he said, "Then, you'll be coming back."

I took the subway back into the middle of the city and went to an agency where they are supposed to help you find a room or whatever. At this place, I was told that they could only help me if I was a student or had a work permit. Remembering that I had seen a sign across the street from the train station, which read Immigration, I went there and told them that I needed a work permit. I was promptly informed that a law had been passed, making it illegal to issue a work permit from within the country. They said that they seriously doubted if I could ever get one in the country. Work permits had to be applied for and received before entering the country. To put it another way, a work permit isn't just something you can walk in and ask for.

What do I do now? I still had $200 more than I need to get back to New York and that might not be such a bad idea. That letter I picked up in the Copenhagen Airport said that I should go to the American Deserters Committee.

CHAPTER X

I did not go there right away because I didn't have any reason to go there. I mean, I didn't come all the way over here just to see American deserters. The immigration people gave me the address. I followed the instructions and when I got there, the Americans were there, all 15 or so of them, sitting around doing nothing. Well, there they were, white Americans, many of them seemed to dislike me. Too bad it's that way, but that's the way it is. As a matter of fact, I try not to dislike anybody. To me people are people first, and whatever else they are after that. There were a couple of teenage girls running around there, and the first thing these Americans said to me was, "Man, you've got to stay away from these here girls. Man, you know when the brothers come here, they only stay a little while and then they leave." Yep, no doubt about it, they were Americans alright. First, they think I want to take their girlfriends. I will, if I want to, in my own good time. Second, they want to get rid of me because I'm black. Ain't that just like white Americans!

In any case they sent me over to Skan, SNCC, and I might add, as quickly as possible. Skan, SNCC, was the Scandinavian Student Nonviolent Coordinating Committee Branch Office, and it was there that all of the black American deserters met. The guy who was in charge of the place was named Richard Rucker, who was from Brooklyn. He introduced me to another guy sitting at a desk whose name was Mark. He was from upstate New York. Richard was married to a Norwegian girl and has lived in Scandinavia for many years. He also lived in Paris before that. Mark left the states to avoid being drafted into the Army. He only arrived in Sweden a couple of weeks before me. Richard was planning to move into a seven room apartment in two weeks. There, he would have enough room for me. He didn't know where I could stay until then.

However, Mark knew a girl with an apartment and thought I might be able to stay with her. So he took me over to her apartment and sure enough, she said it was all right for me to stay there. Mark asked me if it was acceptable to me. It was only a one room apartment with a tiny kitchen and posters of Chairman Mao, Che Guevara, Karl Marx, Lenin and others hanging from the walls. In addition, she was a member of the Communist Party. None of that meant anything to me. I wasn't there to get involved in politics. I only needed a place to stay for a couple of weeks. With this red hot mama walking around the place in various stages of undress, I told Mark that I believe the arrangement was quite suitable. So, he left me there. Whatever did he do that for? There was a big turtle crawling around on the floor with a red star painted on his back and his name was Lenin.

I went back to the train station and picked up my suitcase and came back. I was hungry but she didn't have anything but some kind of caviar that you squeeze out of a tube like toothpaste onto some kind of hard bread. At least, she said it was bread. It looked like and chewed like crackers to me. While I was sitting at the table eating, she brought down a book from a book shelf. Then she sat down next to me at the table. The book looked to me like a magazine with soft covers and was about as thick as a 200-page novel. The title of it was "Puss" (kiss) and on the cover was sketched picture of Dr. Martin Luther King's coffin and kneeling on the floor next to the coffin was a sketched picture of Senator Robert Kennedy who was crying large tears that fell on a rolled and twisted-up American flag which he was holding in his hands. I couldn't read it, but it said something about the American dream. When she turned the first page, there was a group of soldiers marching and at some point during their march; they came upon a nude girl lying in the sand. The soldiers, all with rifle and packs still slung on their backs, took turns in having sexual intercourse with her. After they had done their thing and marched on, the girl lying in the sand remarked, "What lovers. Too bad, they've all got gonorrhea!"

Well, that ought to have told me something right then and there. However, being a country boy from the red clay hills and backwoods of Georgia, I was slow to catch on. Like an old mule, we used to have back home, you first have to hit him over the head with a two by four to wake him up. Then you have to hit him over the head again to get his attention. After that, you have to hit him over the head a third time before you start talking to him.

She wanted to go out and buy cigarettes. I opened up my luggage and gave her a carton. I wasn't letting her get away just yet. Lenin put forth a number of good efforts to climb into my suitcase. Too bad I didn't bring along any turtle nip or whatever they like. Well, pretty soon we got sleepy and got in the bed, or should I just say we got into the bed and the next thing I realized, "Help somebody, I'm being literally raped." What an aggressive girl, and I wasn't putting up any convincing resistance.

Her name was Christina and she was only interested in having sex with men. She cried like a baby when I left and smoked up both cartons of cigarettes. I figured she had been compensated fairly enough. During the next few days, the brothers all got together and started discussing various ways to help me remain in Sweden.

Many of them had deserted from the army in Vietnam. One of them, a guy named Jay, whose home was in Louisiana, was one of the Americans that deserted from Japan through Russia. He said the Russians wanted him to live in Moscow but that it was much too cold there for him. Well anyway, many of them either already had political asylum or were being processed before getting it. So they all decided that the best thing for me to do was put in an application for asylum. This would immediately qualify me for social help. I would be given money by the Swedish government to pay my rent and live there. So I put in an application through the lawyer who was handling all the other guys' cases. I wrote down that I was involved in a Black Power Movement and that it was imperative that I left the U.S. in a hurry because the man was after me. Of course, they found out the truth soon enough or maybe not soon enough. The fact is that, I never even taken part in a demonstration, not that I didn't want to.

While they were investigating me through their embassy or consulate in New York or wherever, I was busy living the good life at their expense. I was going to all the discotheques and making it with all the girls, spending all my money and really just carrying on. Richard and Randi, his wife would receive a check in the mail for our rent and Mark and I would go to the social bureau every

Wednesday to collect our 84 crowns ($16) which we were given to buy food. Every time we went there, Mark would tell them that he needed something, a new coat, a new pair of shoes and a new car, if they would give it to him. Well naturally, they didn't give him everything he wanted. Of course, if you looked like you needed a pair of shoes or whatever, they'd give you a check for as much as they knew it was going to cost, and then they'd tell you where to go and purchase the items.

I never needed anything because I brought with me all the winter clothing I thought I would need. I knew the weather would be very cold weather and sure enough, it was the coldest winter they had had in 25 years. In fact, I felt guilty about the money I was receiving. The lawyer through whom I submitted my application, gave me a card and told me to go to the address on the card and sign up for language school. I did that and started school to try to learn the Swedish language.

Meanwhile, Mark started language training at a different school. The class was made up mostly of people from Czechoslovakia and the Arab countries. There was a Chinese girl from New York whose name was Ada Fung and she lived with her Swedish boyfriend in Gamla Stan (The Old Town). There was a girl from Tampa, Florida named Beth who was married to a Swedish guy and a young guy named Paul Kelly, who was from England and married to a Swedish girl.

The class was 6 hours a day and five days a week. It was conducted by a female teacher whose name was Karin Hendrickson, pronounced Carr-in. She would use a slide projector and tape recorder. A picture would flash over the screen and the tape recorder would say something like, "God dag mitt namn ar doctor Berg," (Good day, my name is Doctor Berg.) "jag ar lakare." (I'm a doctor). The next picture would show the doctor with his stethoscope examining a patient. We would hold in front of us a sheet of paper which had the text of the words being spoken. We were taught lessons that would apply to any situation, such as going shopping, buying a movie ticket, or whatever one might do in everyday life.

After about a month, I still hadn't learned much and was really quite bored. I never liked going to school when I was younger. I spent my last two official years in school in the country, where the teacher was my aunt. She had a big hickory stick in the corner that she used to hit the students when they didn't know the answers to her questions. I was the smartest kid in the class. I had 100% in everything. Not because I was trying to be smart, but because I was trying to avoid having anything to do with that hickory stick. Well anyway, I had learned enough Swedish language to get by in the street, and besides everybody under 30 spoke English. I didn't think I had to talk to anybody any older.

One day, I thought I would take a ride to Finland just to see what I could see, or to see what father fate had waiting for me over there. There was a regular boat line between Stockholm and Helsinki. I went to the ticket office and purchased a round trip ticket and a one way cabin. The price for the tickets was $20 round trip. The boat left at 2 p.m. and sailed overnight and arrived in Helsinki at 9 a.m. the next morning. When I got on the boat, I went straight to my cabin to see who my cabin partner was going to be. It turned out to be a middle-aged man, who asked me in Swedish if I spoke Swedish, then German, then French and finally, Finnish. I didn't speak any of the languages and he didn't speak English. I felt very dumb. Here was a man speaking four languages and I wasn't able to speak any. Most people in Europe speak 2 or 3 languages. I could hardly speak the one language I was supposed to know. In later years, I've tried to atone for this and though I can't speak fluent Swedish, I can understand it quite well and read the newspapers and understand about 90% of what I've read. The Finnish man in my cabin left me to myself. I went back out on the deck to watch the houses and trees that seemed to be growing right up out of the rocks that lined the archipelago of Stockholm. Afterwards, I went into the cafeteria to sit down and drink a cup of coffee.

There weren't too many girls on the boat and the ones there, didn't look too interesting to me. With my danger early warning system repaired and operating after my first encounter with the opposite sex over here, I didn't think it was wise for me to take any new chances. A young fellow came to my table holding a bottle of beer and a glass in his hands. He asked if I mind if he sat down to drink his beer. I said to him "Var sa gos och sitt" (Go right ahead and sit.). He sat down to drink his beer and we started to talk. He also spoke four languages, including English. Since I couldn't speak anything else, we conversed in English. I don't remember everything we spoke about, but most of my questions were about the boat trip, the countries and the people living in them. He told me that he was born in Sweden and that his father was Swedish and his deceased mother was Finnish. His name was Thomas. He was on his way to Finland to visit his grandmother who lived in a suburb outside of Helsinki. A few minutes later, another fellow came along and wanted to sit down and drink his beer. He began by telling us that he was from South America and that he was on his way to Leningrad, where he will attend a Russian University. The three of us sat up most of the night and they kept buying the beer and I kept drinking it. I'm not noted for being a drinking man, although I do drink occasionally. It's not something that I just have to do. I could just as easily do without the beer I had drunk. Although, I wasn't drunk, at one point I had to stop drinking beer because I just couldn't hold anymore. I went back to my cabin to get some sleep. My cabin mate was in his bed and already asleep, so I undressed as quietly as possible and climbed into the upper bunk and lay awake the rest of the night wondering if I was going to be seasick or if Bluebeard or Captain Kidd or somebody equally notorious was going to come along and capture us or something. None of these things happened and we arrived safely in Helsinki the next morning.

I guess I had dropped off to sleep for a while because my cabin mate left and I didn't remember him leaving. There was a great commotion outside and I looked out the door to see what it was all about. Everybody had on their coats and hats and was rushing about, so I figured I'd better get my clothes on and follow the crowd. There might be something interesting taking place and if it was, I'd better go out and have a look. I didn't want to miss anything and sure enough everybody was getting off the boat. I must say that was the smoothest landing I have ever experienced on a boat. Later years, while traveling on the same boat line, they usually just sling it up against the foot of the pier a couple of times and give you a good jolt, just to let you know you've arrived.

Thomas met up with me and asked me if I'd like to come along with him out to his grandmother's and meet his folks and maybe have dinner. I agreed to go with him after leaving my suitcase in a locker in the train station. As we were riding out to his folks' place on a local bus, he pointed out a house to me. There in the middle of town, he said that his grandmother had lived there during the war while the city was under attack by either the Russians or the Germans. I don't remember which, probably the Germans because I don't remember reading where the Russians had any bombs or anything else to fight with during those times. Well anyway, he said that the bombs were falling from the sky and all the people in the building were trying to persuade his grandmother to come with them into the basement of the building to be safe from the bombs. She was very stubborn and refused to budge from the toilet where she was sitting. All of a sudden a bomb fell through the roof of the house and on down through the floor of the toilet and continued on down into the basement where it exploded and killed everybody down there. Meanwhile, his grandmother was still safe and sound sitting on the toilet.

Well, it's like I said, "If God is on your side, you've got it made and you don't have to worry about a thing." We arrived at his grandmother's house and I was greeted very warmly and welcomed. She was one of the sweetest old people that I have ever met. As embarrassing as it was to me, after drinking all that beer the night before, I found it necessary to spend a lot time in the bathroom. We sat around talking for a while and later we ate dinner. After dinner, Thomas escorted me back into the center of town. We then went around town on one of those tramway cars and he pointed out all the interesting sights. Since I didn't have time to read much about Helsinki or the history of Finland, I wasn't familiar with these sites. However, at one point during the tour, my stomach began to send up signals to my brain to get up and get off at the next stop, or face the consequences of messing up the man's bus.

I said to Thomas, "Let's get off and walk, because I like walking." We did and after a while I felt much better and didn't throw up. Thomas was ready to go back to his folks, so he showed me back to the train station and left me there. He said he was going out into the country the next day, and invited me to go with him. I would have gone too, but I couldn't get him on the phone before he left. I left my suitcase in the locker in the train station. Since I didn't have a hotel room yet, there was no need to move it. I just sort of stood around in the station. I wanted to go to Russia and visit Moscow. Walk around in "The Red Square," and have a good look at the "Kremlin" and maybe go inside and shake hands with old Kruschev, if they'd let me across the border. Since I wasn't that close to the Russian border, I stayed where I was. I think it's good to broaden one's scope of the world and try to learn more about other people in other countries.

People were getting off the trains that had come in from Russia and other parts of Finland. They would all come into the station where I was standing and shake my hand, pat me on the back, smile, talk to me and put their hands in my hair. Others would walk past me looking me over and turn around and come past 5 or 6 times. I didn't understand a word of what they were saying. I knew that the Mexican Olympics were going on and that was what they were talking about because they would make gestures indicating big, strong and tall and show what they did. I figured they were referring to the black athletes that they had seen on TV.

Being good natured, I smiled and shook hands. I really must have been a sight to see, at least that's what my grandmother used tell me when I was little. I guess, I must have been the only black person in Finland or the first one they had ever seen. Now that I think about it, I believe the American Embassy there had at that time a black charge d'affaire. I thought they were going to put me on exhibit in a museum somewhere in the middle of town so that everybody would have a chance to gaze at me, the 8th Wonder of the World. There was another fellow there from India or someplace in Asia, but nobody took any notice of him. Well, they just wouldn't leave me alone. I decided to go for a walk or something and maybe try to find a hotel room. I went out in the streets and started walking and I came to a store window where a crowd of people were gathered around watching a couple of TV sets that had been placed there for that purpose. I stepped up behind the crowd and thought I'd watch a little of the Olympics. I could see there were some black athletes performing on the screen. However, as soon as everybody noticed my presence, they all turned around and looked at me and started smiling. I am naturally shy and quickly left the area

It was getting late in the afternoon and I hadn't determined where I was going to sleep that night. After asking around in a couple of hotels and being told that there were no rooms, a man standing near the clerk in one of the hotels, understood and spoke English and offered to share his room. He told me that he had a room there in the hotel, it had two beds in it and that I would be welcome to sleep in one of them. It wouldn't cost me anything. Well, having a suspicious nature and being a New Yorker, I learned not to trust anybody but myself. Whenever anybody started trying to be too nice to me, I would get suspicious because I figure I must have something that they want. I looked him up and down very carefully. He was a nicely dressed fellow, had what I thought was an honest face and a sincere look in his eyes. After I had thoroughly sized him up, I accepted his kind gesture.

We went into the room which was on the first floor and I thought that was good. In case anything started happening to me, I could holler out and maybe the desk clerk could hear me and come to my aid. Once inside the room, his bed was on one side of the room and mine was a safe distance on the other side. I sat down on my bed and he sat in a chair which was placed next to a writing desk and pulled out a bottle of "KOSKENKORVA" (Korrs-skinn-korva), a Finnish vodka and broke the seal on it and offered me a drink. I told him, no thank you. I wasn't thirsty, especially since I drank all of that beer the night before on the boat and was sick all day. Besides, I figured I'd better try to remain alive and in control of all my faculties, just in case.

Just before I left Stockholm, Richard told me that the Finns were a much warmer people than the Swedes and easier to make contact with, but that they might get mad in a hurry and take out their knives and cut each other up when they started fighting. Then, they'd get up and wipe off the blood, shake hands and be tight buddies again. Well, if someone would do that to me, I don't think we'd ever be buddies anymore.

Well, he started drinking and started talking and the more he drank, the more he talked. He told me over and over again about all the terrible things the "Dad blasted" Russians had done to him and his people during the war. Before the battle was over, the Finnish army had let the Russians know that they had been in a fight. Well, his English wasn't good enough for me to understand what they had done to him. He was using just as many Finnish words as English, and still pulling on his bottle, and I was sleepy and nodding off a lot. But sometime during the night, or should I say early morning, he took off his shirt and showed me the wound in his right side where some Russian soldier had run him through with a bayonet. He went on saying very bitterly, what he was going to do to them Russians, if he ever got his hands on one of them.

He never tried to harm me in anyway. I must say, that wound looked to me like the guy who ran him through, must have twisted the knife two or three times after he pushed it into the front and out of his back. To explain it a little better, it didn't look like a wound that a knife leaves after it has been pushed in and pulled out, which would heal leaving a somewhat straight scar. The scar on this guy was about as large as a fist in front and maybe half that size in the back. If it looked as bad on the inside as it did on the outside, well I don't know what he was doing walking around alive. I guess, he had God on his side too.

He finished his bottle and finally went to sleep and I was glad of that because it was around 3:30 a.m. I decided that Finns generally don't like Russians. At 8 o'clock, he got up, washed up and dressed and said that he was going to town to meet with some government officials to discuss the sale of an invention he made. The invention would separate oil from water, and reduce the damages to beaches as a result of oil spills in the ocean.

If I remember correctly, I believe he said that the process had something to do with hanging foam rubber onto fishing nets and stringing the whole thing up and down the coast in the water, and that the water would pass through the nets and the foam rubber would trap the oil. I know that rubber foam does make a good filter. It sounded like a good idea to me and I don't know if he said that he had sold it to the British or was going to sell it to them.

I expressed my gratitude and said farewell. That was the last I ever saw him. Even though he gave me his address in Turku, I never went there. I always had trouble sleeping during the day, so I figured I might as well get up and go out and see what was going on out there on the streets. I went out to the street and saw people moving around and generally going on about their business. Some of them would turn around and look at me, but nothing as sensational as the day before. I guessed they had gotten used to me being there by now. I had my instamatic camera with me and snapped a few pictures. It was much colder in Helsinki than it was in Stockholm. The entire time I was there, it rained mixed with sleet. I was beginning to feel a little hungry, so I thought I should find some place to eat. I remember seeing a sign across the street from the train station that said "City Pukavia Restaurant." I went there and started to enter this fancy looking place, but the maitre d' at the door informed me that in order to enter the restaurant, I needed to be formally dressed. He kindly showed me a place a few doors down, where I could get a good meal. I went into the second restaurant which was a big cafeteria and when I got there, I still couldn't get anything to eat because I couldn't read the menu, I didn't speak Finnish and the woman on the other side of the counter taking the orders, didn't speak or understand English. I'd ask them what they had or tell them what I wanted. They'd smile and shrug their shoulders and wave their arms to indicate to me that they didn't understand what I was talking about.

I stood there for a while and other people would step up and place their orders and receive what they wanted and go on over to a table, sit down and eat. Well, I thought of the maitre d', a few doors up the street who spoke English. Maybe, I should ask him if he would come to the cafeteria and assist me with ordering my food. Just as I decided to ask the maitre d' to help me, a couple came in speaking English. British English that is, they told the woman in Finnish what they wanted. I asked them if they would place an order for me. They did that and I wound up with a large bowl of beef stew. I found a place and sat down and ate. I would have gone back and ordered another bowl, but it was too much trouble. I contented myself with making a couple of trips to the self service counter for coffee and cake. It seemed to be a very international place to me. I mean, there were a number of people sitting around drinking coffee and speaking German or French or whatever. I didn't understand why the personnel there didn't speak English. I know that's the wrong way to look at it. I mean, you can't go into somebody else's country and complain or force them to speak your language. Americans have a habit of doing that. If anything, we should try to learn some of the other languages around the world, at least enough to get by with when you go there. The Swedes on the other hand, would never pass up an opportunity to show a foreigner, and especially an American how well they could speak English. Many of them speak German, as they were under the influence of the Germans during the Middle Ages. I spent the rest of the day walking around and looking around, taking pictures and generally acting like a tourist.

CHAPTER XI

My boat was leaving the following afternoon, so that meant that I needed to look for a hotel. I didn't want to go back to any of the ones from the day before, so while I was sightseeing, I looked around for a hotel as I went along. I didn't see any, but I was lucky to find two young boys who spoke English. They said that earlier in the year, they had an American exchange student living at their house and learned English from him. They directed me to where there was a hotel. There was a guest checking out, just as I walked in. I was fortunate enough to get his room. After I registered, I went up to my room and as I stepped off the elevator, a chambermaid stepped on pushing a little cart loaded with bed linens. I guessed she had just cleaned my room. I went in and thought I would lie across the bed for a while. I guess I fell asleep for a long time, because when I woke up, it was dark.

I got up and thought maybe I'd go down to the train station because I needed my razor and shaving cream that was in my suitcase. I went into the train station's restroom and took a quick shave and replaced my razor into my suitcase. I thought it would be nice to send some postcards, so I went over to the newspaper stand and bought some. The post office which was also in the train station had a table where you could stand and address the card or letter or whatever you were writing. While I was doing this, someone came up next to me and said in English, "Excuse me, but aren't you from the Ghanaian Embassy in Moscow?" Well, that shocked me. I looked up from what I was doing and probably had my mouth open in surprise. There was a well dressed young woman standing there. I certainly was no diplomat and I knew I didn't look like one. I said, "I'm sorry, but I believe you have the wrong person, because I've never been to Moscow."

She smiled and said, "In that case, you look like someone I know." I finished what I was doing and went over to the post office window and she came up and got in line behind me. I turned around to look at the table to see if I left anything over there. I didn't see anything, so I guessed I did not. Meanwhile she smiled continuously. The person in front of me finished and I stepped aside and told her, "You're welcome to go ahead of me if you like, I'm in no hurry." "Oh, thank you."

She didn't have a letter to mail, but I believe she purchased stamps. She stepped aside and began searching for something in her purse. However, just as I had finished my business at the window she managed to finish hers in her purse. As I turned to walk away, she asked very friendly like, "What are you doing in Finland?" "Me? Oh I'm just walking around and looking." "What did you see?" "Oh, I guess I saw everything. You speak English quite well." "Yes, I worked at the British Embassy in Moscow." "Oh excuse me for not introducing myself, I'm Marvin Brown." "I'm Ptirkko Ward. Where do you come from?" "Well, I came to Scandinavia from Brooklyn, New York, but I'm really from Cairo." She said, "Oh Egypt?" "No, no Georgia! Do I really look Egyptian?" "Well, maybe not. Listen there's a restaurant upstairs in this building. Why don't we go there?" I thought about it for a minute. I didn't really have anyone to talk to since Thomas left me here. She spoke perfect English, and it could be nice to sit and talk for a while. "Well, yes that sounds like a nice idea." "It's this way." We walked down to the opposite end of the station and up some stairs and sure enough, there was a restaurant.

We went in and found a nice cozy area in the corner, and she said, "You drink beer don't you? I will order some." Oh, boy here I go with this beer again. Tomorrow, I will have to be on the boat. I just know, I'm going to be sick as a dog. I was too, but not from the beer. I asked her, "Are you going someplace?" "Yes, I'm on my way home." I asked, "Home, where do you live?" "Oh, I live in Lievestuore" "Oh, I see. Well how did you happen to be in Helsinki today?" "I went to the American Embassy." "Oh, really. Were you there to get a job?" "Oh, goodness no. I'm getting married to an American who is in the army." "In the army, I didn't know they had American soldiers stationed here in Finland." "No, no he's not here. He's stationed in Germany. I was there to be with him a week ago. His name is Captain Palk." "When do you plan to get married?" "Sometime during the first week in January, that's when he goes on vacation. After his vacation, he'll have a new assignment in New Jersey."

"I see, well I wish you all the happiness and lots of luck." She said, "Marvin, where do you live? I mean, don't you stay at a hotel?" "Well, yes. I live at a hotel, but I'm leaving tomorrow." By this time, we've had about four beers a piece and she is a little tipsy and really just about lying on top of me with one arm around my neck and one hand holding my knee. At one point, she pulled my head around and kissed me. I said to myself, oh, oh watch out, get back! "Marvin, I have over three hours before my train leaves. So, why don't we go over to your hotel?" I knew it, I just knew it.

Having already gotten burnt the last time I was seduced. I got a bad case of gonorrhea from the young lady I was temporarily staying with in Sweden. I wasn't planning to get burnt or seduced no time in the near future. I thought I should cut this mama loose. Well, maybe we can sit here and carry on this kissing party. I don't see where that can be harmful, but damn, three hours! I started thinking of a convincing way out of this situation and very quickly. I said, "Well yes, that sounds good, but they told me at the hotel that I'm not allowed to have a guest in my room"

She sat straight up and turned to face me with a look of half anger, half shock and disappointment. She said, "They told you that?" "Sure did, that's exactly what the man said." She said something in Finnish that I didn't understand and I guess it's safe to assume that it was a curse word. "Marvin, will you come with me to middle Finland?" "Where's that?"

"That's where I live." "Oh!" "Will you come with me?" "I don't think I have enough money to get there and back" "It's only forty-two marks there and back." "Well, I only have 35 and I'm sure the beer is going to cost half of that." "Oh, I have money in the bank at home. I can give it to you tomorrow, for your ticket back." "I thought the bank was closed on Saturday." "Oh no, it's open all the time. They're open all the time." I knew she's pulling my leg. She would probably get me up there and I'd have to walk back, or worse yet, get me up there and won't let me come back. I'd probably end up stumbling around up there in the snow somewhere, trying to find my way back. Knowing me, I'd probably get lost and in a million years, some archeologist would come along and claim me as being the first skate guard in the history of the world to be found frozen inside of a block of ice at the North Pole.

"No, I think I'll stay here. The weather is quite bad, and the trains might be running late and I don't want to miss my boat." "Oh, Marvin that makes me so sad." Well, I'm sorry but . . ." Then she started crying. "Oh, how could you do this to me? Make me feel so bad like this." Oh, boy, she's really working on me now. Sniff . . . sniff . . . and then a kiss. "You didn't really mean that did you?" Sniff . . . . "Yes, every single word of it." I'm beginning to feel like I've known her too long, and besides this whole affair is getting boring. At long last, it was time for her train, so I escorted her out to the station platform. She said, "Are you sure you can't come with me?" "I'm sure!"

"When will you come to Finland again?" "I don't know, maybe next year." "I'll give you my address and you can write me". I accepted her address and kissed her for the last time. Before she got on the train she said, "I was supposed to come last week, but I was sick with a sore throat and had to wait until now. I'm glad. Otherwise, I never would have met you. Good bye."

Bye! Wow, I thought she'd never get on the train. I probably won't be coming here next year. She probably won't be here either. I wonder why she gave me her address, if she's going to live in New Jersey. It sure didn't make sense to me. I looked at the clock and noticed it was going on eleven o'clock, so I figured I'd better get back to my hotel and try to get some sleep. I went back to the hotel and lay down and went to sleep. I had the strangest dream. It seemed that I was sitting in a chair and the chair wasn't sitting on the floor. It seemed to be elevated up on a platform. There were some flashing lights. Right after that I got the impression of sitting on an airplane watching the sun go down. When I awoke the following morning, I was coughing terribly and my throat felt as if it was swollen inside. I had trouble turning my head. When I tried to talk, I sounded like I was growling over sand paper. To swallow was quite painful and that was bad news as I was hungry. Whatever it's called that hangs down at the top of your throat, had stretched itself quite a way farther down and every time I coughed, it came flopping up into the back of my mouth. I felt terrible. Growing up, I was never this sick. Other than asthma, I have never been sick, except for an occasional cold, not even a headache. When I moved to New York City, I had strep throat for the first time.

I got up and out of the bed, washed up and dressed myself. I didn't know if I should go out and try to find a doctor or wait until I got back to Stockholm to find one. I didn't have any idea how much a doctor would cost in Finland. I was sure that I didn't have enough money on me to afford one. I figured, I'd better suffer until I returned to Sweden. It was another two hours before my boat left, so I went down to the train station and picked up my luggage. Outside in front of the station was a long line of taxi cabs, so I got into one of them, showed my boat ticket, and that made him understand where I wanted to go.

When I arrived at the pier, passengers were allowed to board the boat. I boarded and found a place to sit, and leave my bag. I went to the cafeteria to have a cup of tea with lemon. My throat was in such a bad state that I only drank a couple of swallows. The pain was just too much. I tried to keep from getting sick at one end, to only wind up getting sick at the other. I went back to my seat and stayed there and it was a good thing I did. It was the weekend and everybody from Finland was going over to Sweden or at least, it looked that way. The boat was very crowded because the many Finns who live and work in Sweden frequently take weekend trips home. There are many people who take the trip just for the pleasure of the boat ride, and to buy cheap liquor and cigarettes.

The average price of a fifth of liquor in Stockholm is about $13, but on the boat, you can buy it for half of that. Cigarettes which are about $11 per carton are sold on the boat for $5. The boat finally started moving after it was fully loaded with cars, freight and around one thousand passengers. The seats were something like those on a greyhound bus and joined together in banks of ten. I sat in the middle, as I had no plans to get up and walk around. Sitting in the seat to the left of me was an American who told me that he visited Russia. He said, he was from San Francisco and that he went to Moscow on a train from Helsinki. While he was there, he took many photographs and also had a quickie love affair with a Russian woman. He complained that she was very fat because she ate a lot of potatoes.

He said that the Russians liked American chewing gum. He was very sorry that he only had a couple of packs of "Dentyne" with him when he arrived in Russia. He had given it away. He gave one to the woman that he was involved with and the other to the chambermaid in the hotel where he stayed. He offered to send them some chewing gum through the mail, but they declined his offer. He also told me that on his return trip from Moscow to Helsinki, he had trouble finding a place on the train where he could sleep, because he had arrived at the train at the last minute. He said, the Russians on the train realizing that he was an American, managed to find a place for him.

I could barely talk, but I growled every now and then to let him know that I understood him. At one point, he pulled out his wallet and showed me what a Russian "ruble" looked like. It was about half the size of a dollar bill. He told me that it wasn't legal to bring this money out of the country, but that he managed it anyway and that it was going to be a gift to his uncle who was a coin collector.

After a while, he got up and left his seat. He said, he was going out to the saloon. A little later the man sitting to the right of me introduced himself and we started talking. He told me that he was returning from Estonia where he had been to visiting some relatives. He said that he was born in Sweden, but that his parents had migrated there from Estonia. He then went on to say that the Russians had made it against the law for Estonians, to teach and speak their own language. They had to speak and teach Russian instead. He said that in spite of what the Russians said, the Estonian people were teaching their young children their true language at home. He also said that the people in Estonia expected that there would be a revolution in Russia, sparked by the people, who lived in the southern part of Russia where there is a very strong feeling of nationalism. He said, that as a result of this coming revolution, the Soviet Union would break up into several smaller states or countries. I thought that was all very interesting and I told him so.

The trip dragged on and I suffered on. Sometime during the night, there was a couple over in the next bank of seats making love. There were some passengers who got drunk and lay down on the floor and went to sleep in the middle of the aisle. I wished I could sleep but I couldn't. I did manage to cough enough to keep everyone else from sleeping. We arrived in Stockholm at eight o'clock the next morning. I disembarked and as I walked towards customs, there was a crowd of people waiting for some of the passengers on the boat and one of them was waving to me and calling my name. As I got a little closer, I could see that it was a girl who I had met in a discotheque about three weeks ago.

When I met her, she was with a girl friend and my interest was more directed towards her friend who was occupied. In any case, there she was, baby carriage and all, just standing there waving and calling out my name. I wondered how she knew I was going to get off that particular boat, or how she knew I was coming back today, or as a matter of fact, how did she even know I was gone? I don't remember ever telling her that I was leaving. I tried not to see her because she's too overbearing most of the time. I went through customs. I didn't buy anything, so I kept on through the building and out into the street where the girl was. She kissed me and welcomed me back to Sweden and said, "I called your house and Randi said you were in Finland for three days. I knew when the next boat was coming in, so I took the day off from work and came down to meet you." Well how about that! Why did I give her my phone number in the first place? It never gets a chance to rest. I should have stuck to my old philosophy of "Don't call me, I'll call you." "Yes, I was away for a couple of days."

"What did you go to Finland for?" "Oh, I just wanted to look around." "They have nothing to see over there, only some trees and lakes." "Well, I think it was a very interesting trip." "Why didn't you tell me you were going?" Oh Christ, what is she, my mother! "Well, I neither thought of it nor had the time. Now, if you'll please excuse me." "Wait a minute! You have such a bad cough, aren't you going to a doctor?" "Maybe I'll do that, if I can find one. First, I must get home."

"I'll come with you so I can find a doctor for you." "Well, maybe that's not such a bad idea after all." I had no idea where I should look first. I really needed to go to a doctor. I went home and she was hanging on my coat tail, baby carriage and all. When I arrived home, there was no one there. There was a letter lying on my dresser. I looked at the return address and it was from Bobby. I wrote to him when I first arrived here. Now, he finally answered. I opened the envelope and at the very top in large letters was the word SEX, and directly below in smaller letters it read, "Now that I have your undivided attention." Then the letter starts,

> "Dear Marvin,
>
> I got your letter, and am glad you are having a good time. I hope you get yourself together
>
> So I can come and see you. I finally made Chief at the rink. The bosses are: Nervous Dogherty, Crazy Al and Snootie Gus. Behind that, the rink is going haywire. Butch is still my hockey buddy and he's working in Jessie

Halpern's skate shop. By the way, there were a couple of stewardesses, looking for you, and also a big 747, and the nose on the front of the plane said, "Fly me, I'm Pat." Write soon, Bobby, Your Buddy."

It made me feel better to hear from someone on the other side of the pond. Whenever my relatives wrote me, their letters usually took longer to reach me than anyone else because they either didn't use enough stamps or they didn't use the correct address. The Swedish alphabet has 29 letters in it, including all the letters in the English alphabet. In addition, they have ÄÅ Ö. As I lived in VÅRBERG, which is a suburb in south Stockholm, if you don't make a small circle over the Å so that it becomes A (pronounced AWE) it would be a completely different word and happens to be the name of a town on the southwest coast of Sweden. M y relatives, being country folks, didn't understand that there was a Swedish language, let alone a different alphabet. They always sent my mail to VARBERG in south Sweden.

Ann-Marie was busy in the phonebook looking for a doctor, and her three year old daughter, Elaine, was busy pulling everything out of my suitcase. Ann-Marie found a doctor for me to see. We started out the front door as Mark came in. While Ann-Marie rang for the elevator, Mark said, I see you've got your family with you. "Yeah, I've got someone's family." Ann-Marie gave me directions on how to find the doctor, then, she went home. I arrived at the doctor's office and when he examined my throat, he looked into my mouth and said, "USCH!" which is a word used when describing something disgusting. He then said, "You'll need penicillin." Oh, no not again! "I'll give you a prescription for some penicillin pills and something to wash your mouth out." Phew, that was really close. I went to the drugstore and collected the medicine. I didn't have to pay anything. The Social Bureau pays for the medical expenses and prescriptions for the residents of Sweden. Healthcare in Sweden is free. Normally, whenever someone becomes a resident in Sweden, they register with the health insurance office.

This entitles them to the same benefits as a Swede. They are given an identity card which has their number on it. This number is like a serial number on a motorcycle/car or social security number. It is used for positive identification. The number would include your date of birth followed by four other numbers, for example, if you were born on October 19, 1968, the number would look like this: 68.10.19 6296 and that would be your serial number or ID number from the day you're born or if you're foreign, from the day you register until the day you die. It's more like a social security number. I think it's a pretty good system. I believe it's used in most European countries. I was well again, after one week of heavy doses of medicine.

I decided to go back to school, so I returned and though I was far behind everyone else, I stuck with it. The teacher, who spoke fluent English and French, would conduct the class in Swedish and if a student didn't understand something, she would translate it for the student. As the course progressed, she thought we had learned enough to take dictation. She would read from one of the text books and we were supposed to write as she read. When she corrected my papers, I got a red mark at every other word and at the bottom of the page in red letters was the word FY, which is about equal to the word USCH or how disgusting or the Swedish language will never recover from this. Well, I'd be the first to admit that it's hard to learn another language, regardless of what language it is. The Swedish language isn't the easiest to learn.

It would have been just as difficult for me to learn any foreign language, I only speak English. Occasionally, each person in the class would give a fest (party) and he or she would prepare food from his or her home country. When it was Ada's turn, she made Chinese food. When it was my turn, I went down to a special market where they import a lot of the foods that I'm used to eating. I bought groceries, went home and cooked a big pot of black-eye peas, ham hocks and rice. I fried 3 or 4 chickens, made potato salad and baked biscuits and cornbread. I also made about five gallons of lemonade. The fest was a big success! They just couldn't stop eating, especially the Swedes. They had never eaten food like that before. The average Swede will go shopping every day, including Saturday and Sunday and would only buy one can of something to eat that day. They would go back the next day and buy another can to eat then. Their goal is to keep from spending too much money.

CHAPTER XII

But in the long run, they wind up spending more than they would have spent, if they had bought a couple of sacks of potatoes and a couple of heads of cabbage and maybe some flour and meal. But then too, you would have to know how to cook this type of food. I've never had any trouble, because my grandmother taught me everything – how to cook, clean and take care of myself.

When I was still sleeping at Kristina's place, I usually woke up early in the morning. One morning around seven o'clock I heard a key turning in the door and someone came in and called in a woman's voice "Kristina," at which time I pulled the covers over my head to hide. I then stuck my feet out so that whoever it was would see my feet sticking out and realize what was going on. Meanwhile Kristina was still asleep. The person came in and she saw my feet. She went back out into the kitchen, where she continued to call Kristina.

I woke Kristina by roughly pushing her out of bed and told her to go out there and see who it was. After about ten minutes the woman left and Kristina came back and got back in bed and said, "It was my mother. She only came to bring some fish for breakfast. She wants us to come out to Satra, where she lives and have dinner with her on Saturday."

Well, Saturday came and while we're on our way out there on the subway, Kristina told me that she and her stepfather didn't get along. She said, "We don't like each other." When she was twelve years old, she said her mother married her stepfather and he managed to persuade her mother to send her to a home for girls. He accepted her little brother as a son, as he had a son of his own the same age. He never accepted her. She also said that whenever she visited her mother at home and he was there, he would leave the house the minute she arrived. Sure enough, as we arrived and I introduced myself, he did likewise and we shook hands and he said goodbye to me and walked out the door. I was the last person he spoke to. I don't remember his name, but he was a doctor and was in his mid-sixties. I heard Kristina say he was going across the street to polish his car.

Well, her mother made a dinner of blood pudding and lingon berries, home baked bread and a salad. Just as we finished our dinner, Kristina's mother looked out of the bedroom window, probably to see if her husband was still in the parking lot. She became very excited and ran out of the house, beckoning us to follow her. When we got to the parking lot, Kristina's stepfather was lying on the ground in a position that would indicate that he first sat down and leaned against the car and then slumped over. He wasn't breathing and I couldn't feel any pulse. His eyes were open, but only staring. Kristina's mother sent one of the kids back to the house to bring his medicine. The kid returned with a small zip-up pouch. She opened it and dumped it out onto the ground. It contained close to 100 small bottles each with a different type of pill in it. Her mother searched through the lot and found the bottle that she was looking for. She put one of the pills in his mouth, but he couldn't swallow it. I think he was already dead. Someone called for an ambulance and when it came, they took him to the hospital.

About an hour later, Kristina's mother returned home and announced that he was dead. I had moved in with an African American guy from Brooklyn a couple of days before Kristina's stepfather's death and when I got home, I related what happened. He replied jokingly, "Man something's always happening. First you went to this girl's house and got burnt, then you go to her mother's house and her father dropped dead while you're there. You probably scared him to death. I wonder what kind of story you're going to tell us tomorrow, when you come home."

I was acquainted with two brothers from the West Indies, Noel and Derek. They lived in England for ten years. One day, I asked them whether Sweden would be the country of the future. One of them replied, "Man, if this is the country of the future, you can put me back into the past for two hundred years!" And he continued, "I'm not civilized because I'm from the back bush of Africa and yet they get on the bus and subway and push each other and step all over everybody's feet and never even think of saying excuse me. When old people get on the bus or subway, the young people don't give them a seat and out run them to take the available seats. They've never learned what we call consideration for other people."

I agreed that I had noticed such things. He went on to say, "Man, let me tell you a story. Once a couple was walking down the street up in Norrland and the man waved to someone on the other side of the street. His wife asked, why did you wave to him? The man replied that, oh that was my brother. It's the first time I've seen him in 12 years." If that had been my brother, I would have gone across the street where he was and put my arms around him, shook his hand and stood and talked for a while. They don't even care for their own siblings. Man, now tell me how they going to care for someone else. Man, let me tell you what happened to me once. I was standing talking to a couple of girls one day and a half-drunk man came along and started swinging and fainting towards me like he was some kind of fighter. I told him to go on about his business a couple of times, but he just kept on and finally he hit me. I turned around and clipped him one on the jaw and he hit the ground. Man, someone called the police and all the people walking past on the street stopped to tell the man that it was my fault and to take sides with the Swede and they hadn't even witnessed the incident."

"They are the world's biggest liars." I expressed disbelief and surprise and wondered why they would do such a thing to which he replied, "Well Man, it's like this. To the average man in the street, a foreigner, no matter where he comes from, if he's not a Swede, he's a foreigner. Man, I'll tell you for your own good. You better watch these girls. If you ever go to live with one of them, they can be hot natured and cold-blooded. I lived with a girl once. She got mad at me because I wasn't ready to go to bed when she was. Marvin let me tell you, she put me out of the house in the middle of the night on the coldest night of the year. She thought I was going to come begging on my hands and knees, but it's a poor rat that don't have but one hole to run to. I called up one of my other pieces on the side and she told me to take a cab and come on over. She'd be waiting down stairs. It's a hard country man, and it's bad to be out there in the middle of a cold night with no place to go."

I left the West Indian guys and on my way home, I met an African fellow on the subway. He said that he was going to school to become a doctor and that he had gone to a party over the past weekend and the people at the party were all Swedes. They spent most of the night telling him, in so many words, that as he was African and uncivilized, uncultured and didn't have any industry in his country, he was nothing and they were everything. He went on to say that he lived in a building for students only and that everyone in the building was jealous because he had a two room apartment and they only had a one room. The students from India would yell racist remarks through his door and write insults on his door and run away. He said that his government was financing his studies, but that the Swedes believed that every foreigner here is living off the Swedish government. He wanted to know where I was from. I told him New York City.

He then asked if that was the only town in the states, as every American that he met was from New York City. He was from Ethiopia and had the saddest eyes and so had other Ethiopians I'd met. The next time I saw the West Indian brothers, I related what the African had said to me. They replied, "Well Man, I'll tell you like this, there are Africans and there are Africans. The ones from the front line African countries that had their independence for a longer time. They know how to be cool but the ones from the back line countries that have only been independent for a short time, well they're another story. They come up here from Paris and were probably smuggled to France to try to find a girl to take care of them.

Meanwhile they have to spend a lot of time ducking and hiding from the man because they don't have a visa or work permit, and when they get involved with a girl, they think they own her. That doesn't work up here where women are anything but owned." I considered this all to be an education. The brothers went on to say, "I'll tell you something Man, we were once sitting in a place down in Copenhagen and there was a girl sitting at a table. This African fellow went over and started talking to her. He then went over to the bar to buy some beer. At that time, a black soldier from West Germany walked in and sat down and started talking to her. The African fellow, on his way back with the beer, saw this soldier sitting there and dropped his beer and jumped over the piano with his blade out, screaming, that's my woman man. I'll kill you, that's my woman and he hadn't even talked to her for three minutes. Then you hear stories of girls missing money from their bags while they're dancing at the discotheques. I was in a discotheque one night, Man, and two Africans got into a fight over a girl, so I told them, don't kill each other over a girl, take my girl and I'll go catch me another one. This is Sweden Man. You don't have to fight over no woman. Yeah Man, you got to watch it sometimes."

I told them that these stories were very interesting and that if they had not made me aware of these things, I probably would be ignorant of what is really going on in Sweden. He replied by saying, "Man, you ain't heard nothing yet, let me tell you about those Indians. I lived among them in England, and Man, that is one man you don't trust. If he shakes hands with you, count your fingers cause he might have kept a couple of them. Man, you know that some of them are darker than you and me" I acknowledged that I knew that. "Well Man, they'll call you a black bastard quicker than any white man. I just look at him and laugh. Man, another case of the pot calling the kettle black because I knew how hard he was trying to be white. But wait a minute Man, let me tell you about England. Man, England is the last place to be in the winter time, it's so cold." He would grit his teeth and shiver to impress upon me how cold it was in England.

"Man, the Englishman sits in the pub and drinks beer half the night, because he knows it's the warmest place to be. The most dreaded time of the night is when the barman rings his bell for everybody to drink up, cause it's closing time. He don't want to drink up because he knows he's going home to a cold, cold house. When he gets home he takes the sheet off the bed and hold it over the stove to warm it up, and after he put it back on the bed, he get into the bed with all his clothes on. When he wakes up the next morning, there are icicles frozen on the windows inside the house. If you brush against the wall paper, it's just like brushing against a wet sponge with ice water in it. Would you believe, they put the water pipes on the wall outside the house. I'll tell you Man, if you took a ride through England and then through Germany you would think the Germans won the war. Yeah Man, you wouldn't believe some of the things. For example, there's a street in England where at one particular place along the street all the traffic funnels into one lane, because there stands a wall which they refuse to tear down, just because some saints' donkey took a piss on it a thousand years ago." I thought that was funny so I laughed. "Don't laugh man, it is true."

"I heard a story about a guy who came to Sweden from Africa after having been invited by a Swedish girl who he met when she visited his country. However, the girl lived in Umeå which is about two or three hours from Stockholm, where the International Airport is located. My man having no concept of the geographical size of Sweden, got into a taxicab and gave the driver the address. Upon arrival in Umea, the meter read $50 which he, of course, didn't have. The driver called the police who promptly scooped this poor boy up and put him on the first thing smoking back to Africa. I supposed the cabdriver thought the African happened upon a rich diplomat or a real pasty. Then, there is this brother from the states named Leroy who was married to a Swedish girl and they had a baby together. He was also the father of a second baby with a different girl whose baby was born only two months after the baby by his wife. Leroy separated from his wife a short time later. One day while he was alone in his apartment and feeling rather bored and in want of a little lustful recreation, he called the no.2 girl on the phone and proceeded to tell her what a wonderful, wonderful woman she was and how much he loved the baby, etc. He wondered if she had time to come over so that the two of them could talk about marriage. She, naturally, grabbed up the baby and rushed right over. While the two of them lay in bed, or shall we say while she was convincing him that she wanted to marry him, her baby lay crying on the floor. After they had finished their discussion, she went home and called up all her friends and neighbors and parents to announce that she was soon to be wed to Leroy. However, the next day, old Leroy called her up to tell her that he had changed his mind and really didn't wish to get married after all."

One day while riding a crowded subway, the BO (body odor) was so strong I had to get off at the next stop. It smelled like the end of the month. "Lordag," means Saturday and also means bath day, or so it was said during the middle ages. Lordag is supposed to have been the day for everyone to take a bath and I think it still is. There are a few to whom this doesn't apply. The end of the month is when everyone gets their paycheck. Then it's off to the local Systembolaget or state-owned liquor store to buy a couple of bottles of wine. They become stoned after about three swallows. Half of the Swedes think that Sweden is heaven. Of course, they have plenty of newspaper stories to keep them convinced of that. They'll ask you, "How do you like it here?" and before you can answer, they'll say, "Isn't it better here!

You're not supposed to disagree because the next question will be, "Well, what did you come here for?" Or they would say, "So why don't you leave?" They live like cows in a green pasture, got it made until they reach the slaughter house, or the merchants, or the tax collectors. Sure, it might be better for those people who come here from the Eastern European countries or Africa.

When you go shopping, everything cost twice as much what it cost in New York. For example, the little twelve inch Japanese color TV sets sells in New York for $350. In Sweden they cost $200 more. Meanwhile, the regular 24-inch full size color set will cost $800 or $900. Everybody will rush out and buy one and after they get it home, there's nothing to watch—news, weather and Vietnam (whatever world events that happens to be taking place), an occasional American, French or Russian movie and maybe, a British serial. The stations come on at 6 p.m. and goes off again at 12 midnight.

My brother, who lives in New York, owns a Volvo, a car that's made in Sweden. He paid $3800 for it. If he had brought it in Sweden, he would have paid $900 more. Whenever I was considering buying something, I always compared the prices in dollars and if the comparison indicated that the item would cost more than it's worth to me, I wouldn't buy it. If a Swedish man seemed to be doing a little better than his neighbor across the street, the neighbor would become jealous and go across the street and inquire as to why he bought a new car, when he knew that he couldn't afford it. He will wonder if his neighbor discovered a way to get around old Gunnar Strang (the tax collector) and if he has, he'd like to know what it is. Once, there was a couple who went to Germany and while there, they bought a lottery ticket and won $250,000. When they came back home to Sweden, the tax collector took it all except $50,000. So far I've only met three Swedes who were really ambitious or who showed any noticeable initiative. One was the teacher who taught me Swedish, the other was a lawyer named Bjorn Soderstrom. The third was Anita Seabrook who lives and works in New York.

A magazine once took a survey on how many times a week the Swedish people ate steak. For the first time in my life, I became aware that to eat steak was supposed to be a big thing. In other words, for a Swede, a steak is supposed to mean that he's doing well. For them, a steak isn't a thick cut of beef with a T-bone in the middle. It's in fact, a thin slice of meat with no bone and is cooked in a frying pan on top of the stove. You're supposed to eat it quickly before it gets cold and becomes too tough to chew. Yes, you can buy thick T-bone steaks but at a cost of one arm and two legs. Being raised on a farm, I was conditioned to think that eating steak wasn't anything special, or that it wasn't any different from eating pork. Of course, we kept plenty of meat hanging up in the smoke house and we had cows and hogs in the pasture. To me, meat was simply meat.

Skan SNCC formed a study circle which met once a week to read from the book, "The Wretched of the Earth." I wasn't really interested in this study group, but didn't want to be a bad sport so I went along with the program. One particular meeting was interesting. The discussion was about how the French government, after the war was over, discharged their black African soldiers on the island of Madagascar. These black men served in the French Army and fought during the war. I was never in the army so I don't know what it meant when you're discharged. Anyway, these black soldiers were brought to Madagascar to receive their pay and to be decorated, or at least that's what they were led to believe. However, as soon as everyone assembled, the French didn't bring out the medals and the money. They brought out the machine guns and the bullets and yes, they shot and killed every black soldier present, their last gesture of thanks. It seemed that the French didn't want these black men to return to their villages which were under French control. They thought the blacks, with all of their military knowledge, would start a revolution and demand their independence. That is gratitude for you!

I read a story in a magazine about a guy who had robbed a few places in Sweden. The robber was from some other part of Europe and he wrote that they were the easiest jobs he had ever pulled. He would stand on the corner and wait for the man from the state owned liquor store to go past with the day's receipts in a shopping bag,. The bag could contain anywhere from $25,000 to $50,000. He would then point a gun at him and take the bag. He would leave the country at one end, while the police would be looking for him at the other end. The robber said that if he had waited on that same corner for another ten minutes, the same guy would be back with another sack full of money.

The robber would go through southern Europe on a wild spending spree and after he ran out of money, he'd come back and knock off someone else. He did this a number of times before he was caught. He was sent to prison for three years.

Whenever you visit someone's house and plan to be there for any length of time, you're supposed to take with you a couple of bottles of wine and maybe a loaf of bread and a piece of cheese. Otherwise, they'll think that you came to free load. I know an Ethiopian girl who had been invited over by a family. After she arrived, she was asked by the mother to give the daughter a piano lesson. At some point during the piano lesson, the Ethiopian girl was served coffee and cake. When she finished the lesson and put her coat on to leave for home, the family asked for 2 crowns (50 cents) for the coffee and cake, while the piano lesson was free.

CHAPTER XIII

Mark and I normally went to the social bureau early in the morning. We were always there when they opened the doors at eight o'clock. Recently, however, I had been sleeping late because I was usually out late the night before. Anyway, as I was getting dressed one morning around 9 a.m. to get to the social bureau, the doorbell rang. I opened it, and there stood two men asking for me. I identified myself and they identified themselves as immigration police. The funniest thing to me was the way they carried their badges which were attached to one end of a chain and shoved down into their front pocket, while the other end was attached to one of the belt loops in their trousers. They told me to get dressed and come with them, which I did. They drove me down town to the main police station. There I was shown into an office, where a different policeman of higher rank greeted me and was very friendly. He read from a piece of paper and said that I had a valid American passport and that there was no reason for me to remain in Sweden. I was to be deported as soon as possible, and until then, I would be kept in jail. He reminded me of the executioner reading off a list of crimes from a scroll at a witch burning ceremony during the middle ages.

The two policemen who brought me to the police station were sent back to my house to pack my things. They packed everything including a shopping bag full of garbage that I had sitting next to my bed. I was taken downstairs to a photographer who told me to sit in a chair that was built on a platform. There was a long lever running from the chair out to where the photographer was and every time he flashed off a shot, he would use this lever to swivel the chair around to a different angle. I don't know how many pictures he took, but he photographed me from top to bottom and from every angle you can think of. I was later finger printed and taken to a room and put under lock and key. I was in a jail cell but it wasn't a cell block as I knew them. There was another guy in this room with me. He was from Finland. He said that he had to stay there for two weeks and I can't remember the reason he gave.

Needless to say, I wasn't too happy about being in jail. While I didn't mind being kicked out of Sweden, I certainly didn't like being put in jail. The Finnish guy was trying to talk to me, but I didn't feel like talking to anybody. I was sitting backwards in a chair or sitting with my head and chest resting against the back of it. Apparently, someone had noticed this and thought that I was high on narcotics. A nurse came and rolled back my sleeves to see if I had needle marks on my arms. As far as I was concerned, that was really putting salt into the wound. First, they throw me in the clink and now they think I am a junkie. The Finnish fellow was sleeping on the bed while I was supposed to use a mattress on the floor. I had no idea what time it was because I didn't have a watch and my room didn't have any windows. Having a watch wouldn't have helped because at that time of the year, it was dark at 2:30 p.m. and didn't get light again until 9 a.m. the next morning. I was waiting for them to turn the lights off, so I could go to sleep. They didn't turn the lights off and I never went to sleep. My cellmate was fast asleep. At some point, the door opened and a man came in with two trays of food and said "Ah de tar frukost" or "its breakfast time." I accepted my tray and ate half of what was on it. A short while later, a man came and told me to follow him downstairs. I did and was shown into the office of the man who read the deportation paperwork to me the day before. His name was police assistant Samark and he explained to me that he was only following orders that he had received from the "Utlands-Kommitionen" or immigration department and that none of the officers taking part in the case had nothing personal against me, but were only following orders.

I understood that the police were following orders and thought that was fair enough. I told him I didn't like being kept in jail. He then explained that I was scheduled to leave the next day, Friday. He said that he would try to arrange for me to leave right away. He got on the phone and called some people and called the airport to inquire about when flights were departing for New York. He also said that I could return to Sweden anytime I wished. If I intended to stay in Sweden, I should make sure I had all the proper visas and permits.

I was given my coat and luggage and packed into the back seat of one of those tiny Saab cars. Two plain-clothes cops drove me to the airport which was about 35 miles from town. At the airport, they bought a ticket for me and paid for my luggage and told me that they were going to escort me as far as Oslo, Norway. The airplane captain said that he thought that they should escort me the whole way to New York, because he didn't want the plane hi-jacked to Cuba. I told him that I didn't want to land in the ocean because I couldn't swim. A few weeks before, a Scandinavian plane landed in the bay off San Francisco. The plane took off at 2:30 p.m. and landed in Oslo about 45 minutes later. The policeman got off, and the plane was refueled and repaired. I believe the mechanics changed a part of the number 3 engine.

The plane took off ½ hour later and the sky above the clouds reflected the red sunset all the way to New York, about a 7 ½ hour ride. There were a few white Americans on board and they appeared to be downright annoyed, embarrassed and disgusted because I was on board the plane. They would look at each other and then look at me and frown showing a sour expression on their faces as though they had a bad taste in their mouth.

I don't believe they were aware of my situation and it wasn't appropriate for anyone to explain it to them. Of course, I would have to admit that I wasn't looking my best. I wasn't given any chance to take a bath and try to freshen up. On my way to the airport, I asked the officers to stop at the bank so that I could withdraw the $80 in my bank account. With the $80, I had planned to go to Gothenburg and from there take the boat to England. My brother Homer was stationed in Kent in the U.S. Air Force. Knowing what I have recently learned about the British, they probably wouldn't have let me get off the boat. The officers seemed rather surprised that I had money in the bank.

When the plane landed in New York, it was 5:30 p.m. Swedish time was 6 hours ahead of New York time. As a result, I only lost 3 hours, or maybe gained 3 hours. I'll have to say that I didn't experience any kind of racism while in the land of the Vikings. However, they generally don't like the Finns and a few don't like foreigners. I think the Swedes are really very nice people. I didn't get vaccinated before I left the US or Sweden. Since I didn't have an international shot certificate to show, the immigration agent spent a few minutes harassing me about all the diseases that I might be bringing in the country. He finally said that he wasn't going to vaccinate me and to get out of there and stop wasting his time.

I was holding onto a luggage cart to use for my luggage whenever it came. When it finally arrived, and turned around to load my suitcase, a woman had my cart and was walking away with it. I said to her that I was using it. "Well I'm using it now!" Yep, no doubt about it, I'm back in the wicked city. Once out in the terminal I changed what money I had into dollars and took a cab into Brooklyn. As we came down Washington Avenue to Park Place, the cab driver said he would go around the block because Park Place (the street I lived on) was one way from the opposite direction. When he got around the other side of the block, instead of going the way he was supposed to go, he turned the other way and drove slowly at first, then started picking up speed faster and faster in the wrong direction. So I politely asked him, "Where the hell are you taking me?" He said, "Oh I didn't know, I . . . I . . . I thought this was the way to go." I mean just how smart do you have to be to go around the block? If I had been an out-of-towner, he probably would have taken me all the way up to Buffalo or somewhere just to run up the meter.

I got home and Mama Sara was glad to see me. She said that she kept my room waiting because she knew I was coming back. I wonder how she knew that. I called my cousin who informed me that my grandmother had died while I was away. I also threw out the trash (empty beer cans) that the Stockholm police had packed and that I brought all the way from Sweden

The following Monday morning, I went to Wollman to inquire about a job. Mr. Callender who was one of the foremen greeted me warmly and said that he didn't have any chief openings. I didn't expect that he would, but that he did have an opening for a skate guard and that I was more than welcome to have it. I accepted it and went to the Arsenal to go though the appointment ritual.

When I met with Mr. Veackie, he wanted to know if I was that skate guard who went gallivanting around Europe. I acknowledged that I was, and he then just stared at me, as if to say, what the hell business you got, being over there? Once you've been a chief, and especially for a long time, it's hard to go back to being an Indian, because then you really have to work hard. Of course you have to work when you're a chief too, but the only manual labor is between sessions when you're reconditioning the ice. However, as a skate guard, I was back to skating the sessions, shoveling out the pit, chopping out the pit and all the other dirty jobs. Now that Bobby was my chief, things had really switched around. I really didn't have it too bad, as he usually followed my lead anyway.

It was about mid-season and the time of year when it snows heavy. We really didn't have much time to be idle. One of the guys working in Jessie Halpern's skate shop was a block operator for the Penn Central Railroad. He asked me why I didn't go to Penn Central Railroad and take the test. He said, they really needed people on the railroad. Near the end of the season at the rink, I took the Penn Central Railroad test and sure enough, I got the job. The first thing I had to do was take a physical. The doctor claimed that I had high blood pressure, but that it was no hindrance to performing the duties of the job. Later, I was given rule books to study plus a railroad timetable. The following day at 8 o'clock, Mr. Marconi, who was in charge of payroll, gave me a railroad pass and told me to go down on track eight and get on a commuter train to New Jersey. He told me to tell the conductor to let me off at Hudson Tower, and that he would call the operator and tell him I was coming. Twelve minutes later, I stepped off the train in front of a two story tower. I went in and introduced myself and the two guys sitting there did the same.

The operator's name was Rapid Robert Moran and the other guy was the maintainer and his name was Happy Jack Marlowe. My first two days entailed sitting and observing what the operator was doing, which is called posting. The operator was training me to do the job. Someone would buzz him on the squawk box and give him the train number and the number of the engine pulling it, which would come past next. He would in return relay the message to the next tower. Sometimes, a freight train would go past that was supposed to go down the engine track to Kearney Yard, and the operator would do something with a switch release and rearrange the route so the train could go where it was supposed to go. At other times, he would talk on a short wave radio, to a train.

Every so often, a buzzer would ring and the train dispatcher, who was also the immediate boss, would ask for a report and the operator would give the train numbers and the times the trains went past. The Port Authority Transit Hudson Railroad, better known as the PATH Train which ran from Newark, New Jersey to Manhattan, also ran through the Hudson interlocking. There was also a newly built train which was recently put into service to run from New York to Washington and Philadelphia. It was supposed to have a top speed of 130 mph and looked like a group of airplane fuselages without wings, connected one behind the other. The name of the train was the MetroLiner, but we called it the Super Subway. It was said that it would arrive in Washington, D.C. 18 minutes sooner than an airplane from New York.

On the third day, I was placed in the hot seat. Rapid Robert showed me where to write on the westbound side of the block sheet even numbered west bound trains coming from Portal Tower, and where to write the east bound odd numbers trains coming from Dock Tower or Newark Station, heading into New York Penn Station. Everything went fine until the guy at Dock Tower, whose name was Jerry Mad, demanded to know who I was and started to yell at me. Rapid Robert got angry and had a heated argument with Mr. Mad, then took over the controls for the rest of the day.

After 2 weeks, I was a qualified operator or so we all thought. I was called into the office in Penn Station to take part in a class which consisted of 10 new guys, all involved in learning the book of rules and how to write train orders. The class was held twice a week. At other times, I was sent to Waverly Railroad Yard Tower to post the Waverly 3 shack. It was a shack in the middle of the freight yard and the yard was way out in the back sticks of Newark, New Jersey. The first time out there, it took me three hours to find the place. The tower operator, a middle age man, John Roundlard actually jumped up and down, yelled and screamed at me for being late and refused to sign my time slip. During the course of several visits there, he told me all about his wife and eight kids, what he did on his day off and that he rode up and down the railroad taking pictures of trains and looking for hot boxes. A box or truck is the part under a railroad car where the wheels are mounted. The box becomes overheated when friction is created from the wheels turning and causing the bearings and housing to overheat. If the bearings are worn out and become cherry red, we then have a hot box. Mr. Roundlard also told me that he had at home a number of crossties, a piece of steel rail, a few switch levers and signal lights. I could hardly believe all these things.

I didn't like Waverly Yard because they didn't have automatic signals like the ones at Hudson. You had to walk down the track and throw the switch by hand. One day I walked along stepping on the ends of the crossties and my weight was enough to tip up the opposite end of the ties, someone told me that a coal train had recently turned over there because the beds weren't well secured. I qualified at Waverly 3, just so I could get out of there.

I qualified on the book of rules and there was a job on the bid sheet at Hudson Tower. I put in my bid and won that job. I started to work the 3 p.m. to 11 p.m. shift at Hudson and I worked the 12 a.m. to 8 a.m. shift at the pool filter plant. Two of the guys that were on my book of rules list were working the two towers to the east of my tower. One of them was L.J. Wheeler, who was working Kearny Tower and who had been a football player on the San Francisco Forty-Niners but had to stop playing because he was a hemophiliac. He was about 7 feet tall and weighed a good 225 lbs. The other guy working Portal was Mr. Willie. He had served in Vietnam and this was his first job since he was discharged from the army. Anyway, when train traffic wasn't too heavy, we spent a lot of time on the squawk box talking to each other. One day Wheeler buzzed me, "Hey Brown." "Yeah, "I ain't got nothing to do right now—no trains." "So what." "I want to go to sleep, but I can't." "Do you have an extension cord?" "Yeah, but what's that got to do with it?" "Everything," "What do you mean?" "Take the extension cord and form a circle around your chair." "For what?" "Let the ends overlap each other and make sure you walk in through the opening before you close it!" "What's that gonna do?" "Keep out outside influences!" "What happens then?" "You'll go to sleep." "Brown, I don't believe that, but I'll try it anyway, and if it don't work, I'm going to route one of my freight trains to come over there and knock your tower down." "It'll work."

Half an hour later, he buzzed me back. "Hey Brown!" "Yeah" "Brown I still can't sleep." "You got the wire arranged wrong." "What you mean?" "The vibrations are pointing the wrong way. So, what I do now?" "Take the cord and turn it around in the other direction." The next day he buzzed me back. "Hey Brown." "Yeah, are you some kind of magician?" "No, why?" "Brown, I went to sleep and I slept for an hour and a half." "Oh, yeah!" "Yeah, Brown, the dispatcher was trying to call me. The conductor off the truck train couldn't get me on the radio, so he came up to the tower and beat on the door. That's the only way I woke up." "Is that right?" "Yeah, Brown, I ain't lying, the dispatcher wanted to know where I was. I told him I was in the toilet." "What did he say to that?" "He wanted to know what the hell I was doing in there for more than an hour." "Well, at least it worked." "Hey, Brown." "Yeah." "Where'd you learn that?" "I don't know . . . . read it someplace in a book." "Well, when you go into the movement bureau again throw a spell on W.C. Kong." "How come?" "Cause, I don't like that little son of a bitch.

One Saturday afternoon there was a work train that wanted to work between my tower and Portal, so the dispatcher came on the intercom to give the train orders to me and Mr. Willie. However, Mr. Willie, who was from North Carolina, and even more of a country boy than I am, was also a little slower than I was, plus he had ulcers. This is the wrong kind of job for ulcers. The dispatcher who is short on patience and long on screaming and yelling came on, "Hello Hudson and Portal, are you ready to take this train order?" We both acknowledged that we were. He made the order, "Train order no 19, August 1, 1969, to operators at Hudson and Portal, hold all trains on 2 track, east of signal 66 between Hudson and Portal, made complete at 4 p.m. Ok, Hudson read it back." When you read it back, you must always spell out the date, the name of the tower, the track and signal number, and the time completed. So I did that and I figured that Mr. Willie probably didn't get it all, and that maybe he could pick up the parts he missed when I read mine back. However, after the dispatcher acknowledged me, he called on Mr. Willie, who proceeded. "Train order August 1969, to Hudson and Portal hold all trains, east of Portal between 2 tracks and 66 signals".

The train dispatcher interrupted with a scream, "Willie, goddamn it, Willie that's not what I told you to write. What the hell's the matter with you?" To which Mr. Willie replied, "Nothing!" The dispatcher ended up spelling out each word. I'm supposed to be relieved at 11 p.m. and afterwards, I go straight to my pool job. However, on that same night, the train dispatcher buzzed me and said "Marvin, I just got a call from Ernie Sarkaidie and he isn't coming in tonight." So, I explained that I had to get to my other job at midnight and he replied, "You're not supposed **to** have another job and you can't leave the tower unattended, you'll have to wait until I get somebody to relieve you. There's some kind of federal law which says that a block operator is supposed to have 16 hours free time in between shifts, so that he is well rested when he starts his next shift.

Three and a half hours later at 2:30a.m., a car drove up. Ernie came up the stairs. "Hi Marvin, I decided to come in anyway. Sorry about that Marv. I was hung up with a girl and it was kind of hard to turn her loose." "Yeah, that's fine, but how am I going to get home. There are no PATH trains going by for another two hours."

"Ask the dispatcher to stop 176 to pick you up. He'll be along in 7 minutes." The dispatcher approved the ride on 176, so I got him on the radio and told him he was being stopped to pick up an employee. When I got on the train the conductor said, "Who do you know?" "What do you mean?" "To stop an important train like this, you must know somebody, so I'll ask again, who do you know." I said, "Everybody in the movement bureau!" The following Monday, I buzzed Mr. Willie and asked him, "Hey Willie!" He said, "Yeah." "Is that you?" "Yeah," he barked. "What happened with that train order the other day?" "I don't know . . . the dispatcher was dictating it too fast, anyway, I ain't even thinking about that man. I got 2 trains for you." "Ok, shoot!" "Next up 130 the 4900 followed by 3742 the 105." "Ok, I got it." Somehow he managed to get it backwards. He reported 3742, which is a 4 car commuter train, ahead of 130 which is a 20 car passenger train from Washington.

After he reported the short train first, the train director in A tower which controls the trains coming into Penn Station New York, lined up the railroad to put the short train on a short track, but since the long train was ahead of the short train, it went in on the short or dead end track and promptly ran out of railroad before he got all of his train into the station. The train almost ended up in the waiting room. Later on, I got a buzz from Wheeler. "Hey, Brown." "Yeah." "You hear about Willie?" "No." "They tell me he put a train into the waiting room." "Oh yeah, yeah" "And you know what else?" "No, what else?" All the train directors up in A tower are mad at him. "Oh, yeah!" "Yeah, and so is everybody in the movement bureau." So I buzzed Mr. Willie and asked, "Hey, Willie. What you done?" "I ain't did nothing!" "That ain't what I heard." "They say it's my fault, but I don't work in A tower, I work in Portal." "I hear they all got mad at you." "Yeah that's right, I got to go up on the carpet tomorrow." "Good Luck." "Thanks."

I wasn't such a hot shot operator myself. One evening at the start of the rush hour, or when the trains out of New York are 2 to 3 minutes behind one another, between 4:30 and 6:30 p.m., one train broke down before it got into my interlocking. The train dispatcher said, "Get traffic going west on the east bound track between you and Portal and Dock tower." I did that, by pushing my traffic lever button. Portal can swing his east bound traffic lever around so that it points west. He then presses his button and I do the same, then, I do the same between my location and Dock.

CHAPTER XIV

This process allows everybody to know, without second guessing, which way the trains are going. To put it another way, if someone tries to put a train on a track to go east when all the traffic levers are pulled up to go west, it's not possible to pull up a signal. If a train doesn't get a signal, that train isn't allowed to move. This way it's supposed to be impossible to have two trains going against each other on a collision course. I didn't do anything as bad as that, but the guy who trained me forgot to say that when you run them against the grain, the signals are no longer automatic, meaning that whenever a train goes past a signal it is necessary to pull the signal lever back to neutral and pull it up again for the next train.

So, I pulled up for the first train to go past and all the trains behind the first one were lined up from Newark Station on back past my tower, on back past Portal tower and on back into Penn Station and on out into Sunny Side Yard, Long Island City. Everybody was on the intercom, the telephone, the radio. "Hello Hudson, this is the conductor on the 3733." "Hello, Hello, Hello Hudson, Are you there?" "Hello Hudson, this is the engineer on 111." "Hello Hudson this is W. C. Fields on the Borough Krane." Everybody was calling and my mind was blowing and I just didn't know what to do. The dispatcher rang and W.C. Kong, who was the New Jersey Division Operator came on, "Brown, goddamn you. What the hell are you doing out there?" I told him that for some reason, the trains had all stopped. "Well, Brown, he said, "Why don't you pull up the signals, goddamn it." I pulled up all the signals and sure enough, the trains started moving. The boss called for Joe Fromelt to come and relieve me, and I was told to see Bill Kong at 8 o'clock the next morning.

He said to me, "Brown, don't I pay you to move trains?" Before I could answer he said, "Well goddamn it they ain't moving. Division Headquarters told me to fire you. They wanted to send three people up here from Philadelphia to sit in on your trial. I should suspend you, but you're lucky we don't have anybody else to put there."

I was back to work that afternoon and Mr. Willie buzzed. "That you Brown?" "Yeah," I moaned. "What you done gone and done?" "Nothing," I said dejected. "I thought you had got fired." "No, but it wouldn't matter if I did get fired." "You got another job, ain't you?" "Yeah and it pays more money and I don't have to be going out of my mind either."

The railroad always had a hard time keeping their employees, because they didn't pay any money. Most of the guys quit and go down to PATH headquarters and get hired as conductors or motormen, right away they make $200 a week, plus all kinds of benefits. One summer, Penn Central hired 20 people and before the summer was over, 25 people quit, not only operators but maintenance personnel as well.

Portal tower controls a swing type drawbridge through which tugboats must sometime pass. Sometimes after the bridge has been opened it doesn't always swing back into place the way it should. On one occasion, two maintainers were called to fix it.

One of the maintainers was Happy Jack Marlowe who somehow managed to get his hand caught in the bridge. Meanwhile, there's a train coming out of the New York Tunnel. The second maintainer ran to the call box and told Mr. Willie to put the signal back into Stop position. Mr. Willie being slow to catch on, and not wishing to get into trouble with the train dispatcher, told the guy that the train is supposed to have a clear railroad, no matter what and that he would pull the signal back after the train had gone by. Meanwhile, old 299 or whatever it was called was bearing down on old Jack Marlowe, who is in the middle of the track with his hand caught in the bridge. The guy who was on the call box decided that he was getting nowhere with Mr. Willie, raced down to the tower and threw the signal, and just in time too. The train was so close he could see the engineer's face. The engineer asked over the radio, "What's that fellow doing sitting on the tracks in the path of his train?"

One Monday afternoon, Wheeler buzzed, "Hey, Brown, are you there?" "Yeah," I said. "Hey Brown, let me tell you what happened to me. Know what? I went to Brooklyn Saturday night." "Oh, yeah," I grunted. "How'd you like it?" "Brown, I almost got killed!" Surprised, "Oh, yeah, how's that?" "Willie told me to go to a place called the Flame." "Did you go there?" "Yeah, Willie told me that he was one of the owners, or he hung out there or something." "Yeah, what happened?" "Brown, I was sharp too, I just bought me a new suit and a brand new pair of alligator shoes." "It sounds good!" "Yeah, Brown, I was tough enough and I went in there and asked for Willie." "Did you find him?" "No, Brown. All them cats got up from the bar, and looked at me and asked me if I was the police?" "What did you do then?" "I said, no man, I ain't no police.

I just want to see Willie, and they asked me what I want to see him for?" "What did you tell them?"

"I told them it was none of their business and what did I say that for." "What happened?" "One of them cats pulled out a switch blade knife. I thought it was an axe!" "Did he cut you?" "Hell no, Brown, he didn't get a chance to cut me. You know what he said?" "No. What?" "He told me if I didn't get the hell out of there he was going to cut them gators right off my feet!" "What did you do then?" "Hell, Brown, I put my gators in the street and got to stepping!" "Where did you go then?" "Brown, I went back to Newark. I ain't going to Brooklyn no more. I don't see how you live over there!" "I just don't go to the Flame." "Hey, Brown, call Willie up. I got something to tell him." I then rang Mr. Willie on the outside phone and served as the go-between for Wheeler on the squawk box. I related what happened to Wheeler and Willie replied, "Tell him he went to the wrong place." "Hey, Brown, tell Willie I want to talk to him." "Tell Wheeler not to worry about his gators because if they get cut up, all he got to do is go back down in that swamp and catch him two more. Big as his feet are, it'll take two of them big old gators to make him a pair of shoes!" I relayed the message and Wheeler said, "Brown, tell Willie, I'm coming over to Portal and kick his ass!" "Tell him to come on, I got my 38." Of course, they were only joking and Wheeler was probably lying.

I bid out of Hudson and into a job in Penn Station at Jay O Tower. Mr. Willie bid into C Tower which is also in Penn Station. I qualified after two weeks of posting, and took the 11 p.m. to 7 a.m. shift. The pool was closed and I was back at Wollman, as a day chief from 8 a.m. to 4:30 p.m. My job at Jay O was a much busier job and one that no one else wanted. It entailed mostly moving engines around in the station to make up trains that were scheduled out sometime during the night. This section was the fast end of Penn Station and had so many switches that it was possible to move 3 or 4 trains at the same time. At times, I would forget to pull up a signal. For example, if I failed to pull up the signal and it caused an engine pulling a sleeper car to stop short, the sudden stop would throw all the people out of their beds. If this would have happened, the passengers on New Haven 176 who boarded at 2:15 a.m. and climbed into their beds in the sleeper car could all fall out on the floor and sue the railroad.

Mr. Willie's tower was directly across from my tower and he controlled the Long Island trains. I received my orders from the train director up at the A tower, which is the main tower in Penn Station. Mr. Willie took most of his orders from a Long Island railroad yard master named Cry Baby Eddie Little. One night, I heard the train director tell Willie to reverse traffic between his location and F tower which is at The Long Island City end of the tunnel. The guy who was working F tower was as inept an operator as Willie was. The conversation went something like this: "Ok, when I push my button, you pull your lever over, ok." "No wait, let me push first." "Ok, I'm pushing." "I'm pushing too." "Wait a minute, can't but one of us push at a time." "Well, I'm pulling but somebody ain't pushing." "Yeah, well somebody ain't doing something right." After about half an hour of haggling, they finally got it right. The train director wished he had a tape recorder, so he could take it into the movement bureau and play it back for the boss. I received a phone call from Wheeler about

2 a.m. "Hey, Brown, do you know that 176 is on the ground in Newark, and Willie is screwing up at C tower?" "Yeah, I know."

Meanwhile down at the rink, I'm normally half dead while I'm working. Bobby is alternate chief and Brain is the night chief. When I worked as a skate guard the previous season, after my return from Sweden, Brain would never pass up an opportunity to harass me. He would do such things as send one of his boys out into the park to bring back a shovel full of dirt, or a basket of leaves which he would strew all over the locker room floor and then order me to clean it up. I would have been glad to show him how to be mean and nasty, if that was what he was trying to do.

I had a guy on my crew named Che'o. He was only 18 but he looked five years older because of his size. All the rest of the crew would tease him by calling him Baby Huie. He would get mad and wouldn't talk to anyone for days. But what made Che'o stand out was that he had a Honda 450. He wanted to go California and join the Hell Angels. He also dressed like them. Although he took a bath, or he said he did, he never changed his clothes and whenever he changed the oil in his bike, he would take the old oil and pour it over his clothes. He wore an earring in one ear and frightened the skaters so much that they never broke any rules while he was on the ice.

Many of the rink personnel disliked Che'o because of the way he looked, but I saw him as being just a big kid who didn't really know what he wanted and still had a lot to learn. One day, one of the boys got the key to Che'o's locker, opened it, took out his dirty clothes and dropped them in five gallon bucket and poured two bottles of ammonia on top of them. Someone went out on the ice and told Che'o what happened. Well, he came charging into the locker room mad as a Hell's Angel. He snatched his jacket out of the bucket and put it right on and buttoned it up. He didn't know who he should be mad at, so he was mad at everybody. He pointed his finger at me, and said, "You're the chief, you suppose to see to it that these kinds of things don't happen!"

One morning, I came into work and when I was ready to cut the ice, I found that the jeep was broken and part of the transmission housing was broken away. One of the night crew men said that Brain had been out stump jumping all over the park the night before and managed to get the jeep hung up on a rock. It would run but there was no oil in the transmission. I drove it out to the Randall's Island shops and the supervisor of mechanics was furious. "You guys break more equipment than everybody in all other city departments combined. If I gave you guys a Sherman Tank, you would break that too. I'm going to speak to the Borough Director about all this. That's what I'm going to do!" I told him that the night crew did it, but he only said, "Same old story!" The night crew has always been Wollman's dark horse. Whenever their chief was absent, they would squabble over who was going to be chief for the night. It would end up being all chiefs and no Indians.

One day I came in and everybody from Hollywood had completely taken over the ice, the rink and everything else or so it seemed. They were setting up all their equipment to film some scenes with Ryan O'Neil and Ali McGraw in a movie called "Love Story." The producer said he would use all the skate guards as extras and this meant extra money. At the mention of money, Bobby McDougal hopped all over that producer, flapping his wings like a hungry vulture. The way he was negotiating was like we were the main attraction in the movie.

One of the guys on my crew got a part as a double for Ryan O'Neil. Fast Eddie Parrot did all the fast and fancy foot work in the movie because Ryan O'Neil could just barely stand on his skates. Parrot was paid $120 a day for three days of skating for fifteen minutes. Meanwhile, somebody told me, if I wanted to get into the movie, I should skate alongside the star, and I stuck to O'Neil like fly paper. Sure enough, when the movie came out, there I was, though briefly, skating across the screen next to O'Neil. Vinnie, who was one of the guys on my crew, wore a red sweater which stuck out in the movie like a sore thumb. We were given a plate of food and $15 for our part in the movie. In later weeks, another group of producers came down to make a movie with Shirley McLaine and the supervisor strictly forbade skate guards to talk to or have anything to do with the movie people. That applied especially to Bobby McDougal.

Back on the railroad, I bid out of the Jay O tower and bid KN tower which is in a different part of the station and only handles the Long Island Railroad. The last train would come in around 1:30 a.m. and depending on who the yard master was for the night, I would have a chance to go to sleep. If Cry Baby Eddie Little was working, he would spend the entire night having me move these trains all over the station. He was just like a kid playing with his electric trains, which is precisely what he was doing.

One night I came into KN tower and there was an older fellow there, who said that he was going to work my job and I was supposed to go over to Jay O tower for the night which was a much busier tower. There's some kind of secret agreement between the train dispatcher and the men who have 10 or 15 years on the railroad, to the effect that if the movement bureau calls in an older guy to work a job where somebody had called in sick or something, the old guy would be allowed to work the easiest tower, which was my tower. The dispatcher, who normally worked the easier job, would be sent to the place where it was either too much action or too far out in the woods. That's what happened to me. I worked Jay O tower that night.

The next morning, I didn't get relieved at 7 o'clock because the guy that was supposed to be there called in sick. I had to be at work in the park at 8 o'clock. They kept promising to send somebody and when 9 o'clock came, they still hadn't sent anybody, I said to hell with the railroad and I informed A tower that I was walking out, and wasn't coming back anymore. They had four guys up in A tower and I later learned that they sent one of them down the minute I left. Meanwhile, Mr. Willie quit long before that and went into the barber shop business. I received a letter from the Division Operator's office informing me that I had to appear at a hearing. As far as I was concerned, I had quit and that was that. I was just plain fed up, after all the trouble they put me through. On my days off, they expected me to sit next to my phone all day, just in case they should call me to come to work. Not to mention all those times I had to stay in my tower 2 or 3 hours more than I was supposed to, upsetting my own personal plans.

I felt I shouldn't be making all these personal sacrifices for an organization that didn't appreciate it.

As a matter of fact, the Division Operator really had the attitude that this job was the key to my future. Well, I reckon he soon found out that was not at all the case. The trial, as they called it, took place around 10:00 a.m. in the morning. The Division Operator presided as judge and jury. There were a couple of witnesses present, and the union representative acted as my counselor. Good thing it wasn't a real court room or he would've gotten me hanged. There was this hippie secretary who was supposed to take down everything that was said.

The Division Operator read off the list of charges and proceeded with whatever else he had to say and every now and then, the secretary would get irritated and interrupt with, "Just a minute, you're going to fast, who do you think I am, Della Street sitting here." I would be asked occasionally, if I agreed with what was said, and of course I did. As far as I was concerned, this whole farce was completely unnecessary.

The Division Operator had at one time been a New Jersey State Trooper and was thoroughly disliked throughout the system. He should have remained a State Trooper because he definitely had the disposition for the job. They tell me that the guy before him was twice as bad. In fact, he was in the hospital and sent out a call to all the operators to give blood which he badly needed. The operators sent back a message to him, "Fade him on out, because he wasn't getting a drop of our blood." A pay raise had been approved and made retroactive from January 1st up to the time that I quit. I hadn't received my money. They refused to pay me and right to this very day, they owe me some $350.

I heard one story about a maintainer who had been working on the tracks in the yard in Penn Station and a train came by and cut off both his legs. Within an hour after he had been admitted to the hospital, there was somebody from the railroad office at his bedside, to tell him that he was fired because they couldn't use him any more without his legs. Then, there was another guy who got caught between the couplings of two freight cars down in Waverly Yard. The cars actually coupled together through his body. All the old timers told me to get off the railroad because there was no future in it. So, the railroad and I parted company.

There was one incident that took place which I consider sad as well as unnecessary. Up until now, I hadn't pressed the issue of race or who was what color etc., because to me it's not important. At no time during my career as a skate guard in the Parks Department was race ever an issue. If it had been, I would have been the first to say so. Like I said, to me people are just people. Of course, there were a couple of individuals around the rink who didn't like that I knew how to make it with all the foreign girls from France, England, Finland, or wherever they came from. I would like to think that, that was just plain old fashion jealousy. I had a close friendship with a young Irish girl named Sarah. She was one of a group of British nannies. She would come down to Wollmans with the two kids she was looking after, and as she didn't skate too well, I would give her a lesson or help her around the rink, if I had the time.

WISDOM OF THE TREE
(In Central Park)

Your silent growth I surely heard,
Your limbs support the resting bird,
Your roots nourish our tender earth,
Oh infinite power of the universe.
Dare I tread on the greenest grass,
That raised it head above the dirt, and
Thrust its blade against the sky alert.
To rest my bones beneath your shade,
To lean against your sturdy trunk,
And place an ear against your bark,
To hear the things the Lord has bade.
I touch my head beneath your branch,
And wish I knew the things you know,
Why the multi-colors of your leaves glow,
Your wisdom gained from ages past.
Of gods, of kings and holy things,
I close my eyes, and maybe dream,
That I can see the things you've seen.
You bend and sway beneath the storm,
You thirst for drink on summer morn,
Your growth may stop in winter's cold,
It is surely true, you have a soul.

KATE WOLLMAN
Dear Old Kate

You've taken the best years of my life,
But what have you given me in return
A sheet of ice to cut and pan,
That's built on top of blood and sand.
I've ploughed the snow that nature sends
And frost that grows from end to end
I skate in water or rain above
That drenched the ice a skate guard loves
The pit, is always work to do
Will tax the strength of a weary crew
Tis true o Kate, I'm growing old
Your work is hard, your weather cold
So please, oh please no more demands
Because, I have done the best I can

One Saturday after work, she had more packages than she could carry and she asked me if I would be kind enough to walk her home and carry some of her packages. So I helped carry her packages while she looked after the children. When we arrived at her building on Park Avenue at 83rd Street, we entered the building and the elevator amidst the hateful stares and gawking of the elevator operator, the neighbors and the tenants in the building. I remained at the apartment for about an hour while Sarah was busy fixing food for the kids, washing dishes and generally cleaning up. The people Sarah worked for were British Government diplomats and were out of town for the weekend.

I later left the building amidst the same reception committee. The following week when I saw Sarah again, she told me that, the neighbors and elevator operators all took turns relating to the people she worked for that she brought a Negro into their house. In addition, Sarah was having a serious argument with the woman she worked for on other matters. Unfortunately for poor Sarah, the wife of her employer was an American woman. He was an Englishman and Sarah said he didn't wish to make a big deal out of it, but his wife promptly began to interrogate her about the matter. She questioned her about what her mother, father, sisters and brothers would say, if they all knew she was going out with a Negro.

Sarah replied that neither her parents, her sisters and brothers have any role in choosing her friends or who she went out with, nor had any of her folks received any formal training on how to be prejudiced or racist, and they had no interest in such things. Fortunately for me, I was spared the humiliation of meeting the woman. I don't know what the woman's name was, but unfortunately for Sarah, she was fired and arrangements for her to return to Ireland were made very quickly. Sarah left the following week and not long after that, that particular diplomat and his family moved to a new assignment in Germany.

I had been in the homes of many diplomats in New York City, met and talked with most of them. They were just regular people. All of them were very nice. Of course, most of the bigots were past middle age and once they all drop dead, the country and the world will be a better place for everyone to live in. I say drop dead, because it's not possible to change them. For me personally, I'm not one to sit in some corner with my hands over my eyes and ears crying, "Oh these prejudiced people hate me, I'm being discriminated against." If I can't make it in one place, I'm not nailed down to that spot. I'll most definitely get up and go somewhere where I feel I can make it. If I can't make it in this new place, then I'll just move on. After all there is a whole world out there.

I can remember when I was young and growing up in the south all the politicians that were trying to get elected governor would base their entire campaign on speeches of how bad they're going to treat the "Negras." The one that declared that he could treat them the worse was the guy who usually got elected. The black folks would be the first ones to go to the polls to vote for them, if they were allowed to vote. I guess they just didn't know any better. Many of these same politicians, ancient though they maybe, and that includes their ideas, are still in Washington today, although they have long since out lived their usefulness, such as it was.

CHAPTER XV

Another English girl I knew wasn't allowed to enter the front entrance of the building and ride up the elevator unless she was escorting the children that she was looking after. Otherwise, she would be told by the doorman to use the rear or service entrance. If these girls are good enough to look after these people's children, wash their clothes, cook their food, and clean their houses, I think they should be good enough to ride the damn elevator or use whatever entrance they so choose. These girls are only paid $25 or $30 a week for their work, slave labor if you ask me. And speaking of doormen, they always act as if they own the damn building.

After fifteen years of working as a seasonal worker, I took the civil service test and became a permanent employee even though I had worked full time from when I started in 1964. Civil Service status meant that I was entitled to more benefits and could also take a promotional test. The permanent status was established. My boss and manager gave me the title, provisional supervisor and put me in charge of the Borough of Manhattan at night. I was known as the night rider. In other words, after the Borough Office closed at 5 p.m., there still had to be someone representing the Parks Dept overnight. I drove around Manhattan in a pick-up truck overseeing certain workers at night and making reports on Central Park and other parks in the city. The bosses were out and inspecting everybody's district for cleanness and resolving the problems at the indoor pools and recreation centers and driving the managers home to Staten Island at the end of their day. I got a call to go down to Bowling Green Park to write a report on a packer driver who drove over a man's feet while collecting garbage. One night, I received a radio call to go down to the zoo garage because there was a man walking around in his underwear. It appeared that the commissioner drove into the zoo's parking lot with this official car and saw the man.

The man was drunk and spoke only Spanish, but knew enough English to tell the commissioner, to put the car away himself. Afterwards, they began arguing. There was a man sleeping in the hay loft that heard all the commotion and climbed down to see what was going on. The man from the hay loft worked in that section of Central Park during the day. His name was Anderson and he was a Russian immigrant and lived in the hay loft at night. The commissioner wanted the Spanish guy fired and Anderson to stop living in the loft. Well, the problem with that was every week he was firing somebody. The supervisor, Al Deband who ran Central Park at night, had the Russian immigrant transferred to the north end of the park.

Everyone thought Anderson had no place to live, but as it was later learned, he had been buying up certain types of properties all over Staten Island and owned more houses then any of his bosses. He was forced to resign. Anderson looked like some poor little park worker that had no place to live, but the exact opposite was the case.

I passed the supervisor's test and was promoted from the established Civil Service list. I was assigned to the Five Borough Shops which is the primary shop in the Parks Dept that is responsible for maintaining the swimming pools and ice rinks. My job as technical service supervisor was to survey all 75 swimming pools to determine what repairs were needed. I wrote out work orders for the repairs and hired filter plant operators. I taught them water chemistry, assigned them to a pool, and helped them solve any pool problems that came up. In April when spring began, I would go out to the parks academy in Queens. I would team up with Michael Crescenzo, who is the Director of Training. We start our training with pool supervisors. We would teach them how to oversee the general operation of the pool. Mike gave them all the rules and regulations pertaining to swimming pool operations and I would teach them about filtering and water plant operations and water chemistry. We conducted these sessions on the first day of training. On the second day, we took them out to the pools and demonstrated what we talked about in the classroom. We would show them how a diatomaceous earth system worked and later how an open bed gravity and pressure systems worked. We then took them back to the Parks Academy and give them a written test. By the time the pools opened, we would have trained over 500 people.

Most of the older pools have been renovated over the past twenty years. High Bridge Pool was the first to be rebuilt at a cost of $13 million. When the water was turned on to fill the pool, water escaped from every coupling and joint. The water ran down the Cross Bronx Expressway, down Harlem River Drive and flooded the filter plant. But it didn't run into the pool.

The pipes were made of fiberglass and developed pin-hole leaks that had to be replaced with metal ones, before High Bridge could operate normally. That cost another million dollars. After all that, we still couldn't get enough water to flow though the filters to satisfy the recirculation pumps. So our master plumber decided we should dig up one of the open bed filters to see if there was a problem. And indeed, there were a number of them. We found that the effluent manifold which is the main pipe coming out of the filter to return water to the pool was cracked. None of the mushrooms were screwed into the manifold. They were scattered all over the floor of the filter bed. When the mushrooms are not in place, the sand from the filter escapes into the pool causing the water to be brown and muddy. So our shop (Five Borough) rebuilt one of the six filters and contractors rebuild the other five filters. Some of the valves were clogged and seized up, and they had to be replaced.

Thomas Jefferson Pool was rebuilt at a cost of $12 million. For the first 2 years after the rehab, the pool couldn't be drained at the end of the pool season because the sump pump was too small and our shop had to pump the water out with a suitable pump-out pump. Astoria Pool's new boilers were installed but the pipes weren't installed for the condenser pumps. The pumps remained on the floor rusting as they were never installed. They lay next to the first set of condenser pumps which were also completely rusted out and they were never installed. Astoria Pool is in very bad shape, everything leaked and it was rotted out. It was due for rehab in 1993 but they continued to put it off.

After rebuilding Faber Pool, they gave it back to us with no chemical system for dispensing chlorine into the pool system. The Five Borough shop had to complete the work. The toilets emptied into a septic tank on the pool deck and would occasionally spill over onto the pool deck and over flow into the pool. Nevertheless, our bosses signed off on it. After Lasker Pool in Central Park was rebuilt, our new supervisor of mechanics would not play ball with the construction division, by signing off on an incomplete capital project.

So, he was punished by the powers, John Breen and transferred to Rockaway Beach. But there was no one on Rockaway Beach for him to supervise. So, they hired a provisional maintenance man, so John will have someone to supervise. John Breen hung in Rockaway until he could transfer to a different agency.

One day, the department of investigation called all of us down to their office to talk about all of the construction projects that were incomplete. This required the Five Borough shops, to do repairs. But then the investigation was shut down or hushed up because the mayor did not want a scandal while he was in office. After the East 23rd Pool was reopened, people jumping in the pool were complaining that the pool paint was sticking to their feet.

When the people climbed out of the pool they all had blue feet. After John Breen was vanished to Rockaway Beach they sent in a 22 year old woman to run the Five Borough Shops. She showed up with an assistant. I sat at the desk and showed them how I normally assigned the mechanics to the work to be done each day. As there wasn't someone to supervise the mechanics, that job fell to me for the moment. Or until, they found someone to perform that function.

After I spent two or three days working with the mechanics, by the end of the week my chair was in the garbage, along with my work orders. I had written a work order for a repair to a chlorine pump and other repairs and for some reason, the new chief of operations thought that I was going to file a grievance for the work I was doing outside of my job title.

Nothing could have been farther from the truth, as I had gotten a lot of joy and satisfaction from the work I had been doing. Some of the mechanics had compliance grievances because they didn't like the new boss's method of doing things. The laborers kept her in tears just about every day. The new manager thought laborers were incapable of being bossed around.

She wanted the laborers to drive which wasn't in their job specifications. She wanted the drivers to assist the plumbers and electricians with their work, after they had driven to their job sites. She didn't want to understand that this required a change in title and a higher rate of pay.

One night, Eddie from the night crew was on his way into the building from the ice rink and reached to open the door. Someone inside the building was on their way out pushed the door open and Eddie's hand went right through the glass. His hand was opened up in a number of places and required surgery at Roosevelt Hospital. He's now left with a claw hand for the rest of his life, and a job as a skate guard for the rest of his life. I don't know what else, if anything, the Parks and Recreation Department did for him.

Someone remarked, "How come Marvin Brown can always come back to Wollman and be chief?" Well, I'll just say that a good supervisor knows that a good chief can only make the supervisor look better and a lousy chief will make a bad supervisor look worse. When I first started working at the rink, I always did my job with total commitment and to the best of my ability. I considered myself a good chief. Well, I guess that's about it on the subject of Wollman Rink. My experience there was educational, not only about the job, but also about people and most importantly, about myself. It was a completely different environment than the one I grew up in, on a farm in Cairo, Grady County, Georgia, but that's all another story.

Mr. Sam Sleight has retired. Those who came after him and sat in his chair, behind his desk, in his office, they have exhibited his same type of God complex, duplicated and imitated his style and manner and did everything in their power to try to be just like him. Why can't people stop being somebody else and just be themselves? If the Parks Department can attract more supervisors of the caliber of Mr. Bill Callender, Mr. Joe Defazio and Mr. Bill Kemnitzer, they might just manage to keep their heads above water.

There will be those who will attempt to attack, discredit or otherwise belittle what I have written in these pages. They may feel that they have been maligned. Well, they can rest assured that they have. Even though, I may travel to increase my knowledge of people places and things, I will always remember the experiences I had in Central Park at Wollman Rink and my thoughts will occasionally be of the good times and the good friends I met there.

"Bobby"

Through your strained reputation
As the miser of the park,
May create a situation that
Could leave you in the dark.
When the dollars in your wallet
Mould and turn to dust,
And all your friends are telling
You're not the one to trust.
You should never say tomorrow
For the money you have borrowed,
And pretend you don't know me when you owe me.
If the cigarette you're smoking
Belongs to someone else,
And the girl whose hair you're stroking
Belongs to someone else.
Who cares what people are saying.
May your bank roll never get stolen,
Your Volkswagen keeps on rolling,
And you don't wind up bawling.

McCoy"

If the dozen in your omelet's
Not enough to fill the hole,
Nor the fourteen pounds of bacon
Plus the biggest jellyroll.
When you drink your milk at breakfast
From a twenty gallon mug,
Washing down the ten corn muffins.
That you eat because you love
In a dream, the cook is missing,
And your stomach is protesting,
Scream and scream and scream.
May the corn keep on growing,
The cows never go on strike, and
May you eat all the things you truly like.

"Parrot"

Fastest bicycle in the USA
Spread your wings and fly away,
No one else is fast like you
I wouldn't say it if it wasn't true
Just because you have a pretty hue,
The funniest name I ever heard,
You gave the pack a merry chase,
The day you won the turkey race
You thought to clobber Eddie Mercx,
And try to win your golden crown,
But instead you went to church,
And now you're married and settled down
I hope your bicycle shop's a success, and
Sport the good life in Salt Lake City town.

"Che'o"

When that naked city gas,
Make your Harley run too fast,
You can add yourself some years,
By just shifting down the gears
If you're pushing for the time,
You can stop it on a dime,
And don't forget to let them know,
That you're a stinging Scorpio
When you wish upon a star,
Swinging from your handle bar,
Take along a sleeping sack,
With your mama on your back
I hope your crank case oil is sweet,
And you keep on looking neat,
May your bike keep running good, and
your jeans stick to you like they should.
R.I.P.

"Gill"

Should you remain bitter
Because the world is unjust,
You can't make right the wrongs
That engulf us and be a quitter
Should you strike out
And break their world,
Don't feel sorry for yourself,
Or take it out on someone else,
Remember, as the sun will rise and set,
Fate alone won't substitute for self

"Beno"

Abraham Lincoln was the king of the Jews,
He wore soda water breeches and brogan shoes,
And a beard around his chin,
That made you look like him
You're so skinny you have to tie a knot in your stomach,
To keep your pants from falling down
I'll bet you can stand under the clothes line,
Out of the rain and out of your mind
Do you still grease your hips to keep your hambone from
squeaking,
Edith worships the ground you walk on,
And may you soon realize it and stop fleeing.
R.I.P.

"Angel"

Let sunshine light the path you walk,
And wisdom guide the tongue you talk
To make the most of opportunity,
One must go forth in the world community
May success come and boost your pride,
And may Linda be your bride

Marvin Brown at the Swearing-In Ceremony for adopted sister,
U.S. Ambassador Mosina Jordan at the State Department

Marvin Brown resurfacing ice with a Zamboni at the
Wollman Rink in Central Park

Instructing ice crew on basic ice resurfacing equipment

Model Filter Plant - Used to train Filter Plant Operators
Designed by Marvin Brown and built by the Five Borough Shops

Marvin's adopted brother David

Daughter Saralee skating at the Wollman Rink in Central Park

Tommy, Marvin Brown and Jackie standing at Zamboni garage

The Hitt Family

Johnnie, Marvin Brown, Mosina, David, George and Mama Alice

If I don't see them in the fall,
Tell them for me I love them all.
Forever yours
A soldier of the leaf.